W9-BPM-753

GEORGE
WASHINGTON

PRESIDENTIAL ✦ LEADERS

GEORGE WASHINGTON

JEREMY ROBERTS

LERNER PUBLICATIONS COMPANY / MINNEAPOLIS

For Robert and his friends

The author wishes to acknowledge that his understanding of the Revolutionary War was greatly enhanced by visits to battlefields, museums, and local history collections in New York, New Jersey, Pennsylvania, and throughout New England.

Text copyright © 2004 by Jim DeFelice

Lerner Publications Company
A division of Lerner Publishing Group
241 First Avenue North
Minneapolis, MN 55401 U.S.A.

Website address: www.lernerbooks.com

Library of Congress Cataloging-in-Publication Data

Roberts, Jeremy, 1956–
    George Washington / by Jeremy Roberts.
        p.   cm. — (Presidential leaders)
    Summary: Chronicles the life of George Washington, from his youth in Virginia, through his leadership in the Continental Army, to his years as the first president of the United States.
    Includes bibliographical references (p. 106) and index.
    ISBN: 0–8225–0818–4 (lib. bdg. : alk. paper)
    1. Washington, George, 1732–1799—Juvenile literature. 2. Presidents—United States—Biography—Juvenile literature. [1. Washington, George, 1732–1799. 2. Presidents.]
    I. Title. II. Series.
    E312.66.R625   2004
    973.4′1′092—dc21   2003000395

Manufactured in the United States of America
1 2 3 4 5 6 – JR – 09 08 07 06 05 04

CONTENTS

———— ✧ ————

In 1783 the Revolutionary War was almost over, and
George Washington had just begun the struggle to create
a model of leadership for the young United States.

INTRODUCTION

TO BE KING?

*"The views of Men can only be known, or
guessed at, by their words or actions."*
—George Washington, in a 1799 letter to
Patrick Henry

The general stepped briskly through the side door of the
long assembly hall. The officers, nearly every one in his
command at the New Windsor camp, looked at him in surprise as he marched swiftly to the front of the room strug-
gling to control his anger.

It was 1783, and the Revolutionary War was in its final
days. For more than seven years, George Washington had led
these men through an epic battle against the world's greatest
power, Great Britain. He had made them into a professional
army despite their rags and poor rations. Just as importantly,
he had molded them into real leaders and men of integrity.
Their honesty and fairness, their achievements on the battlefield, their bravery and courage, had given them status that

could not be measured in money. And now some wanted to throw that all away. Some were talking about leaving their country defenseless. Others hinted that their weapons might be turned against the Continental Congress, the central government of their new nation.

A few went even further. An anonymous letter noted that all had great respect for the general. It hinted that if he joined their mutiny, they would follow. While the words were indirect, it was clear that if the general wanted to be king or emperor of America, many of these men would support him.

Had he fought all these years to be king? Had he lived his life by the principles of integrity and honesty to make himself the richest, most powerful person in all the land? As a young man, he'd wanted to be rich and powerful. Here was his chance. If someone had the opportunity to make himself emperor, should he grab it?

The men in the room stopped speaking as he reached the front. They waited eagerly, listening for what General George Washington had to say. . . .

Washington's most severe test and temptation came after years of hardship and trial, just as his greatest triumph was at hand. He reaffirmed his commitment to democracy in the strongest possible terms—and yet would find this resolve challenged again and again.

CHAPTER 1

MAKING HIS WAY

"Utter not base and frivolous things. . . . "
—Young George Washington, copying
out proper rules of behavior

By the early 1700s, Virginia was one of the most prosperous of the thirteen British colonies on the eastern seaboard of America. Although it was first permanently settled in 1607, much of the colony had not been cleared or even mapped out. Most of its land remained wild and untamed. The Blue Ridge Mountains and the Shenandoah Valley were considered the frontier. Farther west, the British were pushing toward the Ohio River Valley. Their bitter enemies, the French, claimed Canada and were moving down the Ohio River Valley from the north.

Most farms in the developed eastern portion of Virginia were small. Tobacco was the main crop. A successful farmer might have a dozen or so cows and a single horse. A one-and-a-half-story building, like the one

George Washington grew up in, was considered large. Slaves, who supplied much of the farm labor, lived in tiny huts and cabins.

Most of the whites had come from Great Britain, and their homeland remained very important to them. It was a source of manufactured goods, a market for crops, and a model of how society should function. Young men from rich and well-off families were usually sent to Britain to be educated. The upper portions of Virginia society reflected British society. A small group of very rich planters, or farmers, sat at the top of Virginia society. They had large estates and a great deal of influence. Below them were smaller-scale farmers and craftspeople. Their wealth and influence varied considerably, generally according to how much property they owned. Then came the indentured servants, who were working off debts or their passage from Great Britain (or both). These servants could be bought or sold, though only for a limited time.

At the bottom of society were slaves. White convicts had been used as slaves during the early years of settlement. By the middle of the 1700s, they were becoming scarce. By contrast, several thousand black Africans were sent to America on slave ships each year during the first half of the 1700s. Most farmers had at least one or two slaves. Several hundred black men and women might live and work on plantations, or large farms. Life for them was harsh. Most lived in small hovels and were punished severely for breaking their master's rules. A large number were treated little better than cattle. Families were routinely split up. Slaves who ran away could be killed if they didn't return to their masters.

*Slaves or indentured servants on a Virginia plantation
prepare recently harvested tobacco to be sold.*

——————————— ✧ ———————————

ROLE MODELS

For many Europeans, the New World of America was a
land of opportunity. A Virginian might earn a fortune, or
at least a good living, with hard work and a little luck. The
Washington family had done just that. They were well off
by local standards. They ranked below the great estate hold-
ers but above most other farmers.

George Washington's great-grandfather John came to
America from Britain in 1657 as an apprentice to a merchant.
After losing his savings in a shipwreck, John had worked and
became a successful landowner, tobacco farmer, and merchant.

George's grandfather Lawrence was an attorney. George's father, Augustine, was born in 1694. Known as Gus, he became a businessman with interests that included an iron mine and a plantation called Epsewasson, located where Little Hunting Creek and the Potomac River meet.

Gus married a woman named Jane Butler. Their children were Jane, Lawrence, and Augustine Jr. Gus's wife, Jane, died in 1729, and soon after her death, Gus married twenty-three-year-old Mary Ball. Mary came from a family that had also done well in America.

George was born to Mary and Gus in February 1732. A sister, Betty, was born in 1733, and brothers Samuel, John Augustine, and Charles were born in 1734, 1736, and 1738, respectively. Another girl, Mildred, was born in 1739 and died the following year.

RULES OF BEHAVIOR
5th – If You Cough, Sneeze, Sigh, or Yawn, do it not Loud but Privately...put Your handkerchief or Hand before your face and turn aside.

George Washington paused as he finished copying the

WHEN IS WASHINGTON'S BIRTHDAY?

On the day George Washington was born, European calendars read February 11, 1732. In 1752 Great Britain adopted the Gregorian calendar. The new calendar dropped eleven days from that year. The change made Washington's birthday February 22. This date is the one usually cited in modern times.

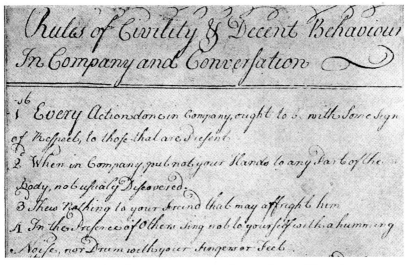

George's handwriting exercise is shown above. The rules
he copied taught him about the social graces of his time.

———————————————— ✧ ————————————————

lesson into his notebook. He reread it, checking his penmanship as well as the words.

*6th – Sleep not when others Speak, Sit not when others
stand, Speak not when you Should hold your Peace. . . .*

George's tutor had set him to work copying the long list
of maxims, or rules for behavior, so he could practice his
penmanship. But the rules themselves were also important
for the boy, who was not yet thirteen. They could guide a
young man to a respectable place in society.

Like other boys in his social circle, George studied with
a tutor. His older half-brothers had gone to England to finish their education, and his father intended to send George
as well. George's father worked very hard and was often
away. He and George did not have a close relationship,
though the boy respected him.

Historians have generally had negative things to say about George's mother, Mary. "History does not always draw noble men from noble mothers," wrote James Thomas Flexner, one of George Washington's most important biographers. Flexner described Mary as self-centered, poor in business matters, and a chronic complainer who belittled her son and his achievements. Signing a letter to her when he was an adult, George described himself as her "most dutiful and obed[ien]t" son. That probably best describes their relationship—formal and strict.

His relationship with his older half-brothers, especially Lawrence, was closer and warmer. Their stories fired his imagination. When Great Britain and Spain went to war in 1740, Lawrence joined the British invasion of the Spanish fort at Cartagena, part of present-day Colombia. Though the attack itself was a disaster, Lawrence returned home a hero to his brother. George loved to listen to his war stories and dreamed of becoming a soldier himself someday.

CHANGED CIRCUMSTANCES

George's young life changed abruptly when his father died on April 12, 1743, after a brief illness. Gus's property, which

———————————— ✧
Fourteen years older than George, adventurous Lawrence Washington was a role model to his younger brother.

included 10,000 acres, the iron mine, and forty-nine slaves, was divided among the family.

As the oldest son, Lawrence received the choicest property, which included the mine and Epsewasson. He renamed the estate Mount Vernon after Edward Vernon, the admiral he had served under in the war. George received Ferry Farm, a property of about 260 acres near Fredericksburg. His father had bought that farm shortly before George turned seven. George also received ten slaves and 2,100 acres of uncleared land. The property was to be managed by his mother until he turned twenty-one. George was far from poor, but there would be no education in England or the other advantages he could have looked forward to if his father were alive.

George continued his education at a local school, learning grammar, logic, public speaking, math, geometry, geography, and history. He was good at math, but his writing style was stiff and awkward—and would be for the rest of his life. His penmanship, on the other hand, was clear and precise—important qualities before the invention of typewriters and computers.

As he grew into his teenage years, George spent more and more time with Lawrence and his new wife at Mount Vernon. Lawrence had married Anne Fairfax in 1743. Anne belonged to an important British family. Her father's cousin was Lord Thomas Fairfax, a British aristocrat who owned much of Virginia's undeveloped land. Lawrence began climbing up the social ladder, and he entered politics. George learned how to behave in proper society from spending time at Mount Vernon. And he longed to have this upper-class life for himself.

"THE WORST ROAD"

George sprouted into a tall, athletic youth. Like his peers, he learned to ride a horse and to dance—important skills in upper-class society. He turned heads with his handsome face and reddish-brown hair.

Like many other teenagers, George longed for adventure. He also wanted to own a large estate and be rich, or at least very well-off. More than anything else, he wanted to be respected. In some ways, he saw wealth and adventure in war as ways to gain that respect.

Ever since he had heard Lawrence's war stories, George longed to join the navy and go to sea. When he reached fifteen, he asked for his mother's permission. She turned to her brother for advice. In the spring of 1747, when George was fifteen, George's uncle told her to say no. He wasn't worried about the danger. He thought the young man would make more money by farming and selling goods.

———————— ✧ ————————

Mary Washington forbids her ambitious oldest son to join the navy.

There is no record as to what George thought of his uncle's concerns, but he did not go to sea. Instead he found another way to earn money: surveying. Surveyors map out property so that it can be bought and sold. Surveying wilderness in colonial America also gave a man the chance to see desirable property before it was claimed. A surveyor might be able to buy land cheaply and sell it later for a profit. Or he could keep the best land for himself, either farming it or building on it and then selling it. This process is called speculating. It was a good way to become rich, though it was also risky.

Along with having good math skills, a surveyor needed to be resourceful and hardy. Roads were little more than trails, and much of the land being surveyed was wild. It was just the sort of job for a young man seeking adventure.

George's father had owned surveying equipment. Sometime in the late spring or summer of 1747, George took out the equipment and began practicing with it. At roughly the same time, Lord Fairfax (Anne's relative) arrived in America to oversee the sale of millions of his acres on the frontier. George was well liked by the Fairfaxes. He was invited to join Fairfax's twenty-three-year-old son George Fairfax and an experienced surveyor named James Genn on a surveying expedition. It was just the chance George had been looking for.

In March of 1748, the group set out with horses and a canoe to survey land over the Blue Ridge Mountains beyond the Shenandoah River. The sixteen-year-old George said the road was "the worst . . . ever . . . trod by Man or Beast." The surveyors often slept under the stars and lived off of the land. It rained often. Once they barely escaped a

*George, shown here on a surveying expedition, used his
new skill to earn money and acquire property.*

———————————— ◇ ————————————

fire in their tent. They met Indians and rough settlers and
woodsmen. George loved it all.

When he returned from the trip, he began earning a
good living as a surveyor. In 1749, the year after his
first surveying trip, he was named county surveyor of
Culpeper County. This was an important post—especially
for someone who was just seventeen. It is likely that
George's family connections with the Fairfaxes led to the
appointment, but his abilities must also have helped.

That same year, George went west again. He was sent
by the company of which Lawrence was president, the
Ohio Company, to survey land for them. The company laid
claim to about half a million acres in the Ohio Valley.

REVERSAL OF FORTUNE

When George wasn't out on surveys, he lived at Mount Vernon with his brother's family. Lawrence had been ill on and off since he returned from the war with Spain. Gradually, it became clear that he had tuberculosis, a serious disease that attacks the lungs and other organs. Seeking a cure, he asked George to accompany him to a spa in Berkeley Springs, on the other side of the Blue Ridge Mountains. The next year, 1751, they went to the island of Barbados in the Caribbean for the same reason. The stormy ocean trip was exciting for George, but there was no cure for Lawrence's disease. He died shortly after returning from the trip.

George returned home sick himself. He had contracted smallpox, a life-threatening disease, on the island. Fortunately, he was able to recover. This left him immune to the disease for the rest of his life. In modern times, children are exposed to the disease by being vaccinated to prevent the illness from striking them.

George returned to Ferry Farm, which he was still too young to take over. The small, infertile farm and his mother's close scrutiny must have come as a shock for the young man used to adventure and freedom.

But even if his circumstances had changed, his ambitions had not. With the help of the Fairfaxes, George won an important appointment as a major in the Virginia colonial militia, its local army. Militias were used for local defense, usually against attacks by Indians. Being an officer in the militia was important politically and often had nothing to do with military ability. Washington would oversee the militia training of an area in Virginia between the James River and the North Carolina border.

BRITAIN VERSUS FRANCE

Since the late 1600s, France and Great Britain had clashed over the expansion of their North American colonies. French settlers in Canada expanded down the Ohio River. Meanwhile, British settlers on the eastern seaboard moved westward into the same area. By 1750 the two nations had already fought several times in North America. Both the French and the British had Indian tribes fighting with them as allies.

In 1753 the French began arresting English traders and settlers in the area between the Appalachian Mountains and the Ohio River. King George II of Britain ordered Virginia lieutenant governor Robert Dinwiddie to send someone to tell the French to stop and to leave the land. If the French did not leave, the British would force them out.

Dinwiddie was an investor in Lawrence's Ohio Company

and knew George well. So it was not surprising that, when George volunteered to take the message to the French, Dinwiddie agreed. But he didn't send the young man simply as a messenger— George Washington also

✧ ————————

Even though Robert Dinwiddie was officially Virginia's lieutenant governor, he was sometimes referred to as the governor of Virginia. The real governor held the office in name only.

went as a spy. Dinwiddie expected him to bring back information about the French forces, so that they could be attacked if necessary. It was to be a long, tough, and dangerous mission.

With the autumn leaves turning bright red and yellow, George set out over the Blue Ridge Mountains. At Winchester he made his way over the Allegheny Mountains, up the Youghiogheny River, and then to the Ohio and Allegheny Rivers. Finally, as the fall weather turned cold, he arrived at the French forts near Lake Erie with his message.

The French answer was clear: they would not retreat. George saw that the French forts were strong and that the French armies were ready for war. He also learned that they were encouraging their Indian allies to attack British colonists. The French were also trying to persuade Indians allied with the British to change sides. War was inevitable. As the snow piled up in the mountain passes, George and his men set out not just for Virginia but for a place in history.

Washington and his companions hurry back to Virginia to deliver news about the French to Virginia's lieutenant governor.

CHAPTER 2

STARTING A WAR

"I had four bullets through my coat, and two horses shot under and yet escaped unhurt."
—George Washington, describing action with General Braddock during the French and Indian War

The cold wind whipped through Washington's heavy buckskin coat. He pushed forward in the deep snow, boots and pants crusted with ice. Despite his great strength, Washington had trouble going on.

Hurrying to deliver the news that the French would not retreat, Washington and his companion, Christopher Gist, had abandoned their horses and the rest of their party several days before. They hoped to make better time by cutting across the woods and frozen streams on foot. They were in such a hurry, they didn't even stop to celebrate Christmas.

When Washington hired an Indian guide who claimed

to know a good shortcut, they thought their troubles were over. But as the trees grew thicker and the snow deeper, Washington and Gist began to suspect their guide was leading them astray.

Washington's feet finally felt so sore he had to stop. The Indian urged them onward. The woods were filled with Ottawa Indians, he told them, who would surely attack them. Come, he said, my cabin is not far away. They could rest there. Finally, the woods parted into an open meadow. The Indian seemed to get a burst of energy and sprinted ahead. Gist and Washington, surprised, trotted to keep up.

Then suddenly, their guide whirled toward them and fired his gun.

"Are you shot?" Washington asked Gist after the bullet whizzed by.

"No."

Neither was Washington. As the Indian ducked behind a large oak to reload, Washington and Gist sprang forward and jumped on him before he could fire again. The men thought the Indian had been sent or hired by the French as an assassin. Gist wanted to kill him, but Washington refused. If they freed him, Gist warned, they would have to run away and then travel all night to be safe. And so they did.

Fearing the French had put a price on their heads, Washington and Gist ducked Indian parties as they made their way home through the frigid weather. When they reached the Allegheny River, they made a raft by cutting logs with a hatchet, only to be trapped in the ice in the water. They had to wade ashore. Finally, they made it to the safety of Wills Creek by January 7, 1754.

A CHARMING SOUND

When Dinwiddie heard George's report on the French, he prepared for war. Dinwiddie appointed Washington second in command of a small group of soldiers. This group was to be sent to an area known as the Forks, where the Ohio and Allegheny Rivers meet. They were supposed to help finish building and then defend a new fort there. The actual commander of the force never arrived, and Washington was left in charge. Washington's orders from Dinwiddie were "to act on the defensive, but in case any attempts are made to . . . interrupt our settlements by any persons whatsoever, you are to restrain all such offenders and in case of resistance to make prisoners of, or kill and destroy them."

Though barely twenty-two years old, Washington welcomed the chance to command. He knew he faced many difficulties. The troops were poorly trained. Money to pay them was scarce, and money for food and equipment was scarcer still. In April he set out with 159 men to the Forks.

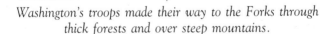

Washington's troops made their way to the Forks through thick forests and over steep mountains.

Washington and his men had to hack a road through the woods for their horses and wagons. Before they reached the Forks, they learned that the French had captured the fort, which they now called Fort Duquesne. With a small group of forty troops and ten Indians, Washington decided to advance toward this French stronghold.

Suddenly his group came across a small French camp in the woods. Washington and his men attacked. Taken by surprise, about a dozen Frenchmen died, and another twenty or so were forced to surrender. Among the dead was Joseph Coulon, Sieur de Jumonville, a French diplomat. His death would soon become a serious problem.

"We had but one man killed, two or three wounded and a great many more within an inch of being shot," Washington told his brother John Augustine in a letter shortly after the battle. "I fortunately escaped without a wound. . . . I heard the bullets whistle," he added, "and, believe me, there is something charming in the sound."

FORT NECESSITY

Following the attack, Washington retreated to an area called Great Meadows, an open field on the western side of Laurel Ridge. Using trees, wagons, and two large ditches, his men constructed a fortification they named Fort Necessity. Forts usually take advantage of geography to make it difficult for the enemy to attack. Fort Necessity did not. It was also too small to hold most of Washington's men. It probably ranked as one of the worst forts in military history. Stubborn and inexperienced, Washington wouldn't listen to advice from the Indians to set up better defenses. It was a decision that cost his men dearly.

This map shows European territories in North American during the conflict
that became known as the French and Indian War (1754–1763).

The French attacked Fort Necessity on July 3, 1754,
and Washington quickly realized that he and his men were
doomed. By nightfall one-third of the men were dead or
wounded. They seemed certain to be overrun the next day.
But then the French surprised Washington by saying that if
he surrendered, they could all simply go home. Washington
quickly agreed. He apparently didn't realize or understand

that the surrender terms included an admission that he had murdered the diplomat Jumonville.

Washington said later that his translator hadn't properly explained the words concerning the diplomat's death. Historians have speculated that the Dutch translator interpreted the word for "assassination" in French into "death" or "loss" in English. It seems likely that Washington thought he was merely agreeing that the diplomat had died, which of course was true. Admitting that he had murdered a diplomat was very different.

Jumonville's death caused a stir far beyond the woods of America. The conflict in America (known as the French and Indian War) became part of a far-reaching worldwide conflict that came to be called the Seven Years' War (1756–1763). France, Austria, and Russia were the major powers on one side. Great Britain and Prussia (part of modern-day Germany) were on the other. The French used the surrender document Washington had signed to convince others that they were morally justified in attacking the British.

"DIE LIKE SOLDIERS"

Though Washington had blundered badly at Fort Necessity, the reports of the battle made him look like a hero, at least to his fellow Virginians. He had faced a much larger army than his own and done so bravely.

The following spring in 1755, Washington joined British general Edward Braddock, who was heading a detachment of regular British soldiers. The British soldiers were called redcoats because of their distinctive red uniforms. They had been sent from Britain to push the French out of the Ohio Valley. Washington joined the general's staff as a volunteer and adviser, traveling with him as the army slowly made its way toward the French. While advising Braddock, he also studied the commander's methods of organizing and leading the army. Braddock's European military experience did not properly prepare him to fight in the American wilderness. But he would not follow Washington's advice on which route to take or what strategies to follow. He also needlessly angered colonists, including Washington, by treating them poorly and criticizing them severely. But Braddock was a forceful and brave commander, and Washington admired him greatly.

Braddock's army passed the ruins of Fort Necessity in

The redcoats' method of marching in long columns
was unsuited to hilly, wild American terrain.

June. Dysentery struck many of the soldiers, including Washington. The illness attacked his digestive system and left him weak and unable to eat properly. But Washington struggled from his sickbed to help the general plan his attack on the French fort.

As they approached Fort Duquesne on July 9, 1755, they were attacked by French and Indian troops. The attack killed and wounded many men. Adding to the disaster, British soldiers mistakenly fired on a group of Virginia militiamen, massacring a number of them. Washington and Braddock worked desperately to stem the chaos during the attack as other officers fled. Four bullets tore holes in Washington's coat, and he lost two horses, but he was unhurt.

Braddock wasn't as lucky. Severely wounded, the general finally organized his troops into an orderly retreat. A few days later, he issued his last orders—Washington would bury him when he died. It was meant as an honor, a gesture to thank Washington for his courage.

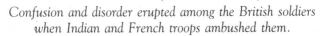

Confusion and disorder erupted among the British soldiers when Indian and French troops ambushed them.

Washington blamed the defeat on the redcoats' panic. He and many others also believed that General Braddock's refusal to use tactics suited to the terrain (such as hiding behind trees rather than marching and fighting in an open area) doomed the army. Roughly two-thirds of the entire force were killed or wounded. It was one of the worst defeats ever suffered by a British army in history. Once again, however, tales of Washington's heroism in rallying the troops spread across the colonies. Following the defeat, Washington returned to Virginia to form a new militia.

REWARDED WITH HARD TIMES

Throughout the French and Indian War, relations between colonial militias and the British army were strained at best. The British treated the colonial soldiers and officers as amateurs and inferiors. Washington had seen the redcoats in action and believed that, in many ways, they were no better than the colonials.

He especially resented the British commanders, since they refused to recognize his rank as colonel. Captains and majors, who normally were under a colonel, showed him no respect. The prejudice and poor treatment damaged Washington's pride and ego. It was particularly unfair to him, since he had demonstrated his courage under fire. He had also seen firsthand that many British officers were cowards and inept.

The prejudice was also dangerous to the army as a whole. A lack of respect could lead others to doubt commands on the battlefield, resulting in disaster. By not following orders, a lower ranking officer could lead his men into a dangerous position, or he could fail to help others when it was needed.

Washington had other problems to deal with. Ordered to protect settlements on the frontier, he spent much of his time just keeping his militia together. Attacks on colonists by Indians in the Ohio Valley and the Allegheny foothills took many lives. For much of the war, Washington had too small a force to stop them.

In late fall of 1758, the British launched a major campaign under General John Forbes against Fort Duquesne. Washington's Virginia militiamen joined the redcoats for the assault. As the army moved northward to attack, disaster struck. A large group of Washington's men mistook another company of Virginians for the enemy. Washington managed to stop the murderous gunfire only by rushing between the two lines of soldiers. When the heavy smoke from the muskets cleared, fourteen men were dead and another twenty-six were wounded. Washington was unharmed.

A short time later, the British learned that the French were retreating. Washington, promoted to a temporary rank as a regular British army general, led redcoats and militiamen in a four-day march to Fort Duquesne, only to find it in

Washington, age 25

————— ✧ —————

embers. The French had burned the fort to prevent its capture and had left the Ohio Valley.

While the war would continue for two more years, Washington's role had come to a close. He had had enough. It was clear that there would no longer be much fighting in his area. He was fed up with the British, drained by the war, and his business affairs needed attention at home. He wrote a letter to the officers who had served under him in the army, thanking them for their service. "If I have acquired any reputation, it is from you I derive it," he said. "I thank you also for the love & regard you have all along shown me. It is in this, I am rewarded."

LESSONS LEARNED

Washington learned invaluable lessons during the French and Indian War. Many were about the best tactics to use in battle. He also learned how to raise an army and win its respect. Most of all, he learned how to improvise and make the most of poorly trained men and small amounts of supplies.

Washington had learned something else. He resented the fact that Americans were treated as inferiors by the British. His anger simmered, even as he turned his attention to business, politics, and love.

CHAPTER 3

HUSBAND AND REBEL

*"Give me leave to add, as my opinion, that
more blood will be spilt on this occasion . . .
than history has ever yet furnished instances
of in the annals of North America."*
—George Washington, writing to a friend in 1774
about Parliament's actions against Massachusetts
following the Boston Tea Party

The twenty-six year old who returned from the wilderness battlefield towered over most of his fellow Virginians. Standing a little over six feet three inches tall and weighing about 175 pounds, Washington had the body of an athlete. He had blue-gray eyes and an intense stare that convinced people whose gaze he met that they were the center of his attention. His reputation as a soldier was widespread. While the war had taken a toll on his business interests, he had many influential friends. He was also single and, therefore, a very eligible bachelor.

Some years before, Washington had met Sally Fairfax. She was the wife of his close friend George William Fairfax, the man with whom he had taken his first surveying trip. He probably fell in love with her, and she was also very fond of him. But it seems unlikely that the two ever became more than close friends. That friendship aside, Washington did not seem to have had many close relationships with women until he began seeing a Virginia woman named Martha Custis around March of 1758.

Martha was a twenty-five-year-old mother of two. She had been widowed the year before. Almost as soon as Washington met her, he decided he would marry her.

Little is known for certain about Martha's ancestors. Her father, John Dandridge, was a county clerk. Her family was probably not wealthy until she married Daniel Parke Custis in 1749. Custis was the son of a wealthy Virginia landowner, who left most of his estate to him. Martha gave birth to John "Jackie" Parke Custis in 1754 and Martha "Patsy" Parke Custis in 1755. When Daniel died, she became one of the wealthiest single women in Virginia. Her

————————— ✧

Wealthy and charming, Martha Custis made a fine match for a young hero like Washington.

estate was estimated at over 23,632 pounds sterling, which is the modern equivalent of many millions of dollars.

George and Martha married on January 6, 1759. Soon after, Washington left for Williamsburg, Virginia's capital.

WASHINGTON IN LOVE

Historians say that Washington developed what might be called a crush on Sally Fairfax soon after he met her when he was sixteen, even though she was married. His fondness continued and possibly grew over the next decade.

If Washington wished for something more than friendship, he seems to have decided by 1758 that this could not be. By then, he had begun to think about marrying Martha Custis. In a letter that fall to Sally, he admitted that he was in love, though he was coy about whether it was with "Mrs. Custis" or another unnamed woman. The playful nature of the letter allows for different interpretations of it. Many, though not all, historians think that Washington may have been saying he was still in love with Sally.

Historians have been frustrated when researching how Martha and George felt about each other. Martha destroyed most of Washington's letters to her after he died. Such letters might have contained hints of passionate love, friendship, or disagreements between them. Washington rarely revealed his deep feelings and thoughts to anyone. So, for the most part, descriptions of their emotions toward each other can only be guesses.

On the whole, the Washingtons seem to have had a good marriage. Washington said that marriage led to happiness, and it seems likely he felt this about his own marriage.

He had been elected to the House of Burgesses, the colony's local legislature, or the part of government that makes laws. Virginia, like most of the other colonies, had its own legislature, elected by property-owning men. But the real power in the colony belonged to a governor appointed by the British government. Local laws and even the governor's decisions could be overruled by the king. The British government also controlled the colonies' dealings with each other and the outside world.

Washington proved to be an able representative, though he rarely took a leading role in debates. Others who served with him, including Thomas Jefferson, noted that Washington spoke little but that his opinion could convince many others. Comparing him to Benjamin Franklin, the great American inventor, patriot, diplomat, and statesman, Jefferson said, "I never heard either of them speak ten minutes at a time, nor to any but the main point which was to decide the question. They laid their shoulders to the great points, knowing that the little ones would follow of themselves."

At the same time, Washington and his new family moved from Ferry Farm to Mount Vernon. Washington's mother was still at Ferry Farm, which had legally become Washington's property. She did not want to leave—and he didn't want to live with her. He did, however, recognize his duty to take care of her and so let her stay. He leased Mount Vernon from his sister-in-law Anne, who had remarried and moved away. He began rebuilding and expanding his new plantation.

The war hero settled down to the life of a country gentleman. Washington was never an avid churchgoer, though he often attended church to talk politics with friends and neighbors after the service. He liked to play cards, and his account books contain many references to the small sums he won and lost in card games. Friends and neighbors thought highly of him, and he had a reputation for honesty. While still ambitious, he did not fall victim to greed or act in ways that others could criticize. Washington considered his character one of his most important assets. He had occasional fits of anger but worked hard to control it.

A FARMER AND EXPERIMENTER

Agriculture was a major business in Virginia in the 1700s. Washington wanted to make Mount Vernon as profitable as possible. He studied a book entitled *A System of Agriculture or a Speedy Way to Get Rich* and experimented with various farming methods. He invented a new plow and planted a large vineyard, trying to make wine. Like many of his neighbors, he grew tobacco to sell to Britain. But in 1765, he

———————————————— ✧ ————————————————

Washington became the official owner of Mount Vernon in 1761, after the deaths of Lawrence's widow and daughter.

decided that it was difficult, if not impossible, to make much money from tobacco. He began growing wheat and corn in large quantities, selling them in America for a better profit. By 1770 he had made Mount Vernon into an efficient farm, even though its poor soil and the attention Washington spent on other endeavors limited its production.

Washington's other business interests included a fishery and a mill. He also bought land in the west, hoping to make money by selling it for a higher price later on. He knew speculating was risky. He sometimes referred to these ventures as "lotteries." But Washington also believed these risks were important to take if one wanted to be wealthy.

GATHERING CLOUDS

Following the end of the French and Indian War, differences between Great Britain and her American colonies began to grow. The colonists objected to the high taxes and restrictive economic policies the British Parliament imposed on them. The colonists saw these as unfair and unnecessary. The British government wanted to tax the colonies to pay off debts from the French and Indian War. It also severely limited the colonists' trade, so goods had to be bought and sold as England dictated. The colonists also resented the fact that they had no representation in Parliament. Many of them were becoming tired of having fewer rights than the citizens back in Britain enjoyed.

As a farmer, businessman, and politician, George Washington was deeply affected by these conflicts. His ability to make a living at Mount Vernon was hurt by British taxes. Washington also resented the way he and other colonials were treated as second-class citizens.

Washington's decision to grow crops that could be sold locally was probably made for business reasons. But it also reflected a change in his thinking. He and many others were coming to view Britain as a hindrance, if not an enemy. Their future lay in America, not Britain.

In 1765 Washington wrote a letter to his London agent, who sold his tobacco and took care of other business interests for him in Britain. Washington complained about the problems he had encountered selling tobacco. Toward the end of the letter, Washington veered into an attack on laws passed by Parliament to tax the colonies, including the Sugar and Stamp Acts. Washington, like many others, believed that taxes should only be imposed by governments that were elected by its taxpayers. Since the colonists were not represented in Parliament and their local governing bodies had not authorized the taxes, they felt they should not pay the British taxes.

"This [unlawful and unfair] method of Taxation," he wrote to his agent, was "a direful attack upon [the colonists'] liberties." Washington wanted his agent and other merchants to put pressure on the king and Parliament to change the laws.

BREAK WITH THE MOTHERLAND
Colonial protests against the Sugar and Stamp Acts led to the lowering of the sugar tax and the repeal of the stamp tax in 1766. Still attempting to make the colonies pay for their defense, Parliament passed another series of laws in 1767. Known as the Townshend Acts, the laws required British troops to be housed by colonists and introduced a new series of taxes, which colonists bitterly protested.

Like many colonists, Washington and his circle of friends were becoming angrier and angrier with the British government. He told his friend George Mason in a letter in 1769 that "no man sho[uld] . . . hesitate a moment to use a[r]ms [to defend his rights]."

The Townshend Acts were repealed in 1770 but not in time to prevent the Boston Massacre, when a group of colonists and British soldiers got into a fight. Five Americans were shot and killed by British troops. In 1773 Parliament passed yet another unpopular law affecting the American colonies. The Tea Act imposed duties, or taxes, on tea and gave a monopoly to the British East India Company, in effect forcing colonists to buy tea only from them. When the governor of Massachusetts attempted to enforce the law, an angry crowd boarded ships that were loaded with tea in Boston Harbor and tossed the tea over-board. Known now as the Boston Tea Party, that protest on

——————————— ◇ ———————————

Onlookers cheer as colonists disguised as Mohawk Indians pour tea into Boston Harbor in 1773 to protest British taxes on tea.

December 16, 1773, showed how angry many colonists had become with British tax and trade policies.

The British Parliament clamped down. It passed a series of laws, known in the colonies as the Intolerable Acts, which were designed to punish Boston and warn the other colonies against similar acts. Redcoats moved into Boston to enforce the laws and to seal off the city from the other colonies.

The colonists were inflamed. "The Parliament of England," said one of Washington's fellow Virginians, Landon Carter, "have declared war against the town of Boston." Washington did not approve of the destruction of property that took place during the Boston Tea Party. But he declared the British reaction "despotic," or the sort of highly oppressive action a tyrant would take.

Many of Washington's friends were talking about a complete break with England. Historians have debated Washington's feelings about this. His business dealings seem to indicate that he felt a peaceful settlement would be reached. On the other hand, he insisted that colonists were entitled to their rights, and he was prepared to use force to uphold these rights. And he helped organize a militia that was intended to do so. Any use of force would mean a serious break with the mother country, and it seems likely that Washington knew this.

In the summer of 1774, the First Continental Congress, a meeting of all colonies (except Georgia), was called to discuss a united protest of British policies. Washington was selected as one of Virginia's representatives. The Congress agreed to boycott, or refuse to buy, British goods the next year—and planned more drastic steps if that didn't work.

Colonists shot at redcoats as the British retreated from Lexington back to Boston in April 1775.

THE TASK OF COMMAND

As British soldiers led by General Thomas Gage took over Boston, Washington helped organize and supervise militias in Virginia. News came of a fight between a force of British soldiers and Massachusetts militiamen in Concord and Lexington. On April 19, 1775, Gage had tried to seize a store of American arms outside Boston by force. In the fights that followed, seventy-three British soldiers were killed and about two hundred were wounded. Forty-nine colonists died, including many innocent civilians, and nearly as many were wounded. These skirmishes—now known as the Battles of Lexington and Concord—would become famous as the start of the American Revolution.

When Washington heard the news, he at first worried that the British would move against his Virginia militias. He was torn between attending the planned Second

Continental Congress in Philadelphia, Pennsylvania, and staying home to command his colony's forces. Finally, he decided to go to Philadelphia. On May 4, he boarded his horse-drawn carriage and headed north.

After the British soldiers returned to Boston, local militias and other volunteers from nearby colonies surrounded the city. The Continental Congress voted to take command of these forces and create a Continental Army. It was a declaration of war against the motherland, though not yet a declaration of independence from it.

Washington wore a military uniform to the Second Continental Congress, an obvious sign that he was ready for war. He also wanted to remind delegates of his military record and probably to hint that he hoped to lead the army.

Historians disagree on the details of the debate over who would lead the new army. It seems probable that Washington was always a front-runner for the post. His exploits in the French and Indian War were well known. He had more experience organizing an army than anyone on the continent. He was an important man from a wealthy colony. He had a reputation for honesty and fairness. Finally, he was a member of the Congress, well known to most of the representatives.

On June 14, 1775, Massachusetts representative John Adams rose in the chamber and began talking of the need for a commander in chief who could direct the army as Congress's representative. As he began to praise the individual he had in mind without naming him, Washington left the room. He knew Adams was about to nominate him, and he wanted others to feel free to discuss it. It was exactly the sort of conduct expected of a gentleman.

When it came time for a vote the next day, it was unanimous. "I am truly sensible of the high honor done me in this appointment," Washington declared in a speech accepting the post, "yet I feel great distress . . . that my abilities & Military experience may not be equal to the extensive & important Trust: However, as the Congress desire it I will enter upon the momentous duty, & exert every power I possess." He also said he would serve without pay.

A day or two later, Washington wrote a letter to his wife using one of her nicknames, Patcy. He claimed in the letter that he really didn't want the job. "You may believe me my dear Patcy, when I assure you, in the most solemn manner, that, so far from seeking this appointment I have used every endeavor in my power to avoid it." But it seemed to be his destiny as well as his duty, he told her, and he could avoid neither. A few sentences later, he told his wife that he asked for a new will to be drawn up "as life is always uncertain."

Within days he left to organize the army on the outskirts of Boston.

*George Washington took command of the Continental Army
in the summer of 1775.*

CHAPTER 4

DEFEAT AND TRIUMPH

"I am mistaken if we are not verging fast to one of the most important periods that ever America saw."

—George Washington, to his brother John Augustine Washington, describing events in 1778

Washington rose on the saddle of his horse, looking out over his army. His men were situated along the Harlem Hills north of New York City on Manhattan Island. In the distance, he could see five British frigates in the East River. The ships had sailed up the river the night before, on September 14, 1776. For the past hour, the British had been hurling cannonballs at Washington's soldiers near Kip's Bay. A fleet of barges began to appear from behind the ships. The British were sending four thousand men against a weak spot in Washington's line, guarded by only a few hundred soldiers. Once the British landed, they could easily surround his army.

Washington quickly gave orders for another group of troops who were positioned in the city to fall back to stronger positions, as they had planned. Then he spurred his horse to take charge of the front lines himself.

FOR INDEPENDENCE

The past six months had seen many changes in America. Washington organized the army around Boston and equipped it with cannons from the captured British fort of Ticonderoga in upper New York. At the same time, he encouraged American forces in northern New York to invade Canada. He even asked Britain's colonies in the Caribbean to join the Revolution.

Any hope for a compromise with Britain was dashed by King George III's harsh reactions to the Americans. He saw the colonists as spoiled children. Washington wrote to his friend Joseph Reed on January 31, 1776, that he hoped Congress would not be "duped" by representatives of the king. Washington hoped that everyone would realize that the only way freedom would be guaranteed would be by creating an independent country.

The Continental Congress wasn't duped. On July 4, 1776, the delegates from the colonies

✦ ———————————

George III had been king of Great Britain since 1760.

In this famous painting, The Declaration of Independence, *artist John Trumbull depicted the signers of the important document.*

officially declared the colonies a united, free, and independent nation. On Washington's order, this Declaration of Independence was read to all the troops.

The surprising strength of Washington's army around Boston forced the British to retreat. They sailed out of Boston Harbor, planning a new strategy. As the summer of 1776 grew warmer, both sides eyed New York City as the next great battlefield.

When the attack finally came at the end of August, British soldiers numbered thirty-two thousand, many more than were in Washington's army. After landing on Long Island, the large force broke through Washington's defenses on August 27 at Brooklyn Heights. Washington kept his army from being destroyed thanks to a brilliant retreat. His troops entered New York City, which at the time included only the lower tip of Manhattan Island. They also took up positions north of the city. Then they waited.

Washington and his troops were forced to abandon Long Island after the British routed them from Brooklyn Heights.

A NEW KIND OF WAR

General Washington had already realized he would lose the battle for New York. But he also knew he had to lose carefully if the war was to continue. Washington had come to a radical conclusion about the war he was fighting. He knew it would be difficult or perhaps impossible to defeat the British in most battles. The British used hired troops from Germany in addition to their own men. They were well equipped and could muster up large armies for individual battles. What they could not do, however, was be everywhere in America at the same time. Nor would they be willing to fight forever.

"On our side the war should be defensive," Washington wrote to Congress's leader, John Hancock, as he waited for the British to attack Manhattan. "We should on all occasions avoid a general action or put anything to the risk unless compelled by a necessity into which we ought never to be drawn."

Washington's strategy did not mean running from the enemy or refusing all fights. If he lost or even avoided too many battles, his men's morale would be sapped, and his army would dissolve. Civilians would think the cause was hopeless, and the Revolution would end.

Even now that war raged, not everyone in America wanted to fight Britain. In fact, historians have generally estimated that for much of the war, those who truly supported the Revolution made up only about one-quarter of the population. Another quarter of the population were Tories, or people who were loyal to the British. The rest—perhaps nearly half the population—did not feel strongly one way or another. Washington recognized that he needed American victories to influence these people to support the Revolution.

He also knew that he had to keep hurting the British army until its leaders felt that waging war was too costly. Washington's strategy in New York City, for example, was to abandon it rather than have his army destroyed. But he only retreated after showing the British that his men would not be beaten easily.

In modern times, this strategy is accepted military practice. It has been used in several wars and continues to influence generals. But in 1776, it was as revolutionary as the Revolution itself.

FIGHTING THE REVOLUTION

Just like present-day soldiers, the Revolutionary army's soldiers relied on guns for much of their fighting. But their weapons were very primitive. British and American soldiers mostly used smooth-bore muskets. These guns were loaded shot by shot from the mouth of the barrel. Even a marksman was lucky to hit what he was aiming at in battle. To be effective, muskets were usually grouped and fired together. Rifles, which use a rifled, or grooved, barrel to spin the bullet, were much more accurate. Though their numbers were small, special companies of riflemen were formed and played an important role in some battles.

The British were feared for their use of bayonets, long knives (usually sharpened on both sides at the tip) attached to muskets. The troops would often charge with bayonets after firing one or two rounds. Especially early in the war, American troops generally lacked the equipment to match this.

Cannons were important weapons for both armies. They could be loaded with cannonballs or grapeshot. Grapeshot consisted of a container of smaller

Most American soldiers carried muskets.

In this battle scene, three straight lines of British soldiers advance toward American forces.

─────────── ✧ ───────────

bullets or shrapnel, which spread out when fired, just as a shotgun shell does today.

Contrary to popular opinion, in most major battles, American soldiers did not fire their weapons from behind fallen trees or rocks in the woods. At least at the start of a fight, men would march forward in lines or wait in an open field while the enemy approached in similar lines. Usually there would be one or two lines behind a front line, which might kneel to give the others a chance to aim as well. When the two groups were close to each other—thirty or forty yards was considered ideal—the commanders would give the order to fire.

In theory, one line of soldiers could move back and reload while another line fired. In reality, battles were often very chaotic. Exact procedures differed from unit to unit, even in the highly regarded, professional British army.

CHAOS, ANGER, AND A SMALL VICTORY

On September 15, British troops landed at Kip's Bay on the East River side of Manhattan. They overwhelmed the Continental Army's poor defenses. By the time Washington reached his men, they were running away in confusion.

"Take the wall!" he shouted to some as they fled. "Take the cornfield!"

But most of the poorly trained and poorly equipped soldiers didn't listen. As the British fired their cannons, Washington wheeled his horse back and forth across the fields. He drew his pistol and even beat some of the men to get them to turn and fight. Finally he managed to get a few hundred to make a stand. But a sudden charge by the British sent these men running in terror without firing a shot. At that point, legend says, Washington lost his temper.

"Are these the men with whom I am to defend America!" he raged. He paid no attention to the hail of enemy bullets that flew all around him. His aides had to grab hold of the reins of his horse and pull him away.

Despite the cowardice of some of the American troops and the overwhelming numbers of British, Washington managed to regroup his army farther north on the island. The British concentrated their next attack on the city to the south, losing their chance to crush the Americans.

The next morning, the attack began again. British troops massed south of the American defenses. As the British moved forward, their buglers began sounding not a battle charge but the tune used at fox hunts. They were taunting their enemy.

With this insult ringing in his ears, Washington sent a force under the command of Lieutenant Colonel Thomas

Knowlton to meet the British. Even though Knowlton's attack did not go exactly as planned, the British troops he met turned tail and ran. This small victory cheered the Americans. It was an important boost on a difficult day and helped stall the British attack. A stalemate set in—the redcoats controlled New York City, and Washington's army controlled the northern part of the island.

A HANDS-ON GENERAL

As Washington reorganized his defenses, he worked to improve how well his soldiers followed his command. "The loss of the enemy yesterday would undoubtedly have been much greater if the orders of the Commander-in-Chief had not in some instances been contradicted by inferior officers who, however well they mean, ought not to presume to direct," he told his troops. Following orders in battle was basic to a professional army. But this idea was still new to the volunteers in the militias and Continental Army fighting under him. One of Washington's biggest problems was the lack of good officers, especially at the lower ranks. "I have neither seen nor heard of one instance of cowardice among the . . . troops where they had good officers to lead them," said Nathanael Greene, one of Washington's most capable and trusted subordinates.

"Washington was not the kind of executive who sits behind an empty desk as details are smoothly handled by subordinates," points out biographer Flexner. "Only when physically separated from the Commander in Chief could aides—or for that matter, major generals—do much altogether on their own. And, wherever Washington acted, he dominated." Washington was what in modern times is called a hands-on leader, someone who got very involved in the details of his army.

Though he worked all his life to keep his temper in check, Washington occasionally raged in times of extreme stress, such as during a battle. Many of the incidents took place when others had failed to live up to his standards, such as when soldiers acted like cowards or when his officers failed in their missions.

DARK DAYS

In mid-October, the British began a fresh round of attacks. Washington retreated north to White Plains, New York. The British followed and at one point threatened to overwhelm the Americans. But then suddenly the redcoats withdrew. They changed their strategy and invaded New Jersey.

Though it had survived the fight, Washington's army had been badly battered. It was short on basic supplies, including ammunition. Men slept in tents or out in the open between battles. They were often without food and lacked proper clothing and boots. "Almost everyone has heard of the soldiers of the Revolution being tracked by the blood of their feet on the frozen ground," wrote Joseph Plumb Martin, a soldier who fought in New York. "This is literally true and the thousandth part of their sufferings has not, nor will ever be told." Martin cited one march to battle in which one-quarter of the men wore only shirts "to cover their nakedness."

The weather turned frigid—snow was on the way. Some soldiers deserted. Worse, the enlistment terms of many soldiers were either expired or would expire at the end of the year. Simply keeping the army intact became a monumental task for Washington. As biographer Douglas Southall Freeman puts it, "To call [Washington's] situation desperate would have been to brighten the picture."

The British left New York and pushed into central New Jersey. The redcoats were on their way to Philadelphia, the base of the Continental Congress. Once the Delaware River froze, they could march across and attack. Even if the Congress escaped, the blow might be fatal to the Revolution.

Washington's military strategy didn't seem to be working. His army was falling apart, and the British seemed to be able to march wherever they wanted. He needed a victory not just to rally his men's morale, but to prove to the Americans that the Revolution could be won. He decided he had to take a gamble.

CHRISTMAS VICTORY

On December 22, 1776, American troops in New Jersey captured a man acting suspiciously. They thought he was a British spy and took him directly to General Washington's headquarters in eastern Pennsylvania. Washington questioned the man himself. Then he ordered his guards to march him to the sentry house and lock him away.

Unknown to the guards, the man wasn't a British spy—he was part of Washington's own secret service, an American agent who had been spying on the British. Washington had asked the agent for a full report on the defenses in nearby Trenton, New Jersey, manned by the German troops the British had hired. What he heard filled him with hope. The British forces were obviously unprepared for an attack. Many of the officers had left the area for Christmas. Washington had a daring plan: he would

To take advantage of the enemy's unpreparedness on Christmas 1776, Washington and his troops crossed the Delaware River in a snowstorm.

————————— ◇ —————————

launch a surprise attack on Trenton while the German troops slept off their Christmas celebrations.

As Christmas Day turned to Christmas night, a storm broke on the nearby Delaware River. The wind whipped the waves, snow pounded downward. In the midst of it all, Washington loaded his troops on small boats and crossed the icy river. It took until four A.M. for the troops to get across and into formation.

Washington rode his horse back and forth along the lines as the men marched toward Trenton. "Press on, press on, boys!" he shouted. As the sun passed over the horizon, they were eight hundred yards from the city defenses. Except for a handful of sentries, or lookouts, the enemy soldiers were still asleep.

The Americans paused and made a line to attack. Their first few volleys that morning missed because they were fired from too far away. But that didn't matter—the American troops charged forward as their cannons began booming. They killed or captured nine hundred enemy soldiers. Washington's daring plan was a great success.

SUCCESS—AND MORE DEFEATS

"I have the pleasure of congratulating you upon the success of an enterprise," Washington wrote John Hancock and Congress the next day, telling him of the rout. The victory, along with another daring attack at Princeton, New Jersey, the following week, pushed the British back toward the Hudson. Philadelphia was safe, at least for the time being.

The battles shook British morale and weakened support back in Parliament for its war policies. They were the first major battles that Washington won, proving that Americans could defeat the British army. But they did not, by themselves, change the course of the war. In fact, the following year the British marched into Philadelphia.

But this time, Washington's overall strategy was starting to work. In late 1777, an American victory at Saratoga in northern New York ended a British plan to cut the colonies in two along the Hudson. It also helped convince the French to lend the Americans badly needed supplies.

Besides his military battles, Washington had to fight political ones as well. He had to beg Congress and the state legislatures to pay his men, and he pressed for supplies and weapons. And in 1780, Washington was betrayed by one of his own generals, Benedict Arnold. Arnold was a hero of Saratoga and an important general whom Washington had supported and recommended for promotion. But Arnold grew dissatisfied with Congress and the Revolution. He plotted to turn over West Point, a fort along the Hudson, to the British. When his plot was discovered, he deserted and changed sides.

Arnold's betrayal must have hurt Washington deeply. But characteristically, Washington did not show any emotion when he found out about the plot. He moved quickly to reinforce the defenses Arnold had harmed and stop further damage.

As the war continued, Washington shared many of the difficulties his men faced. When his army camped at Valley Forge, Pennsylvania, during the winter of 1777–1778, he lived in a tent until huts were built for all of his men.

There were limits, however. Once the huts were constructed at Valley Forge, he moved into a nearby farmhouse.

————————————— ◇ —————————————

During the harsh winter at Valley Forge, American soldiers faced cold, hunger, disease, and injury.

Martha joined him there, as she often did when conditions allowed. He also had his own bed transported from headquarters to headquarters. "Washington did not dine sumptuously... but he never seems to have gone without food, nor does he appear to have suffered any shortage of tea or coffee," notes biographer John E. Ferling.

FRENCH HELP

As the war continued, important foreigners joined the Continental Army. The most famous was the Marquis de Lafayette, a French aristocrat whom Washington treated like a son. Baron Frederick von Steuben, a Prussian soldier, helped train solders. His methods greatly improved the army's ability to operate as a unit during battle.

The French decision to help the revolutionaries was one of the biggest changes in the war. Along with supplies, the French sent a fleet that challenged British ships, cutting down British mobility.

More and more, keeping the American colonies seemed to the British to be unworthy of their blood and effort. But the British didn't give up. They started a new campaign in Georgia and the Carolinas in late 1778 and won victory after victory. Washington sent Nathanael Greene, one of his trusted officers, to lead the fight there. At first, Greene seemed to have little success, and the Americans continued to fall back. But the general was following Washington's strategy. He attacked the enemy and quickly retreated. The British army gradually lost its strength as it stretched out to follow the elusive Americans.

The British army could capture any large city on the continent that it wanted. But it could not eliminate the

Many of the battles in the Revolutionary War took place in the northeastern part of America.

rebellion. No amount of British victories would convince Washington's army to surrender. British politicians were coming to see that the cost in money and lives for holding on to the colonies was too great. The tide in America had turned against them.

Victory looked like a sure thing. But then in the winter of 1780–1781, the army Washington had built so tenaciously over the past five years deserted him.

CHAPTER 5

MUTINY, DICTATORSHIP, VICTORY

"It is easier to divert from a wrong, and point to a right path, than it is to recall the hasty and fatal steps which have been already taken."

—George Washington, describing how he had headed off a mutiny, in a 1783 letter to Alexander Hamilton

On January 3, 1781, Washington opened a dispatch that had arrived for him at his headquarters in New Windsor, New York. The first words filled him with anger and dread. More than one thousand soldiers near Morristown, New Jersey, had mutinied, or revolted. They had taken cannons and started marching toward Philadelphia, where the Continental Congress was meeting. Disaster loomed.

The soldiers had a long list of grievances. Some were angry that they had not been paid for a year. Others believed their enlistments (terms of service) had expired, though their officers disagreed. Congress had tried various schemes to raise money, but resources were scarce during the war. Worse, Congress lacked the authority to tax people directly to raise money. It tried authorizing the states to raise money on their own, but this didn't work any better. Poorly fed and equipped, the troops were tired of promises—they wanted action and planned to force Congress to help them. They had already killed one officer who had tried to stop them and wounded another.

Washington had long argued with Congress to get the men the pay and supplies they deserved. But a mutiny could wreck not only the army but the entire Revolution. While his first impulse was to ride to New Jersey and quell the revolt quickly, he decided to proceed more cautiously. He sent officers to find out whether or not the troops near him supported the mutiny or not. And he sent instructions to General Anthony Wayne in New Jersey to keep the men from attacking Congress. He told Wayne not to use any force. He was worried that doing so would cause others to rebel as well.

At the same time, Washington sent urgent pleas to state legislatures for more supplies and funds. "It is in vain to think an Army can be kept together much longer, under such a variety of sufferings as ours has experienced," he wrote.

Soon after this, officials from the Continental Congress and the Pennsylvania government met with the mutineers in New Jersey. Eventually they agreed to several demands, including allowing about half of the men, whose enlistments were up, to leave the army. In the meantime, the mutineers turned over two British spies who had come to persuade them to change sides. With elected officials involved and the men's loyalties clear, Washington did not interfere.

On January 15, however, another group of soldiers in New Jersey rebelled. This time, Washington moved more forcefully. He sent General Robert Howe and several hundred men to "compel the mutineers to unconditional submission. . . . If you succeed in compelling the revolted troops to a surrender you will instantly execute a few of the most active and incendiary leaders."

Howe surrounded the rebels and forced them to give up. Following Washington's orders, he had two men shot by firing squad. "The existence of the army called for an example," Washington explained later. The mutinies ceased. At the same time, efforts were made to keep the army better paid and supplied.

VICTORY AT YORKTOWN

As Washington was putting out the mutinies in New Jersey, his troops in the South won a major victory at Cowpens, North Carolina. It was the start of a season of victories under Greene, who wore out the British forces under Lord Charles Cornwallis. Greene summarized his strategy in one sentence: "We fight, get beat, rise and fight again."

In the summer of 1781, Cornwallis retreated to Yorktown, Virginia. Then Washington moved his main army south. The French navy cut off a British ship packed with troops in September. Cornwallis was doomed. Washington, with an army from France assisting, pressed in.

The British held on. Washington joined in the fighting,

and he even supervised a bayonet charge by his men. "Sir," said an officer named Cobb as bullets flew, "You are too much exposed here. Had you not better step a little back?"

"Colonel Cobb," answered Washington, "if you are afraid, you have liberty to step back."

The only ones stepping back were the British. On October 19, 1781, George Washington sat atop his horse and waited as a deputy sent by Cornwallis came forward to surrender. More than seven thousand redcoats emerged from their positions to give up a short time later. As they marched forward, their bands played "The World Turned Upside Down," a song whose title showed how strange they found it to be surrendering.

This painting by John Trumbull, Surrender of Lord Cornwallis, *depicts the British surrender at Yorktown in 1781. Washington is shown in the background on a brown horse.*

NOT OVER YET

The surrender at Yorktown in 1781 marked the end of the major British military campaigns in America. Washington had destroyed a sizable portion of the British army. Still, British forces remained in New York; Charleston, South Carolina; and several other smaller cities and strongholds. It was clear, however, that Britain could not win back the colonies without a massive effort. In early 1782, the British Parliament voted in favor of peace.

But in America, it wasn't clear that there would be peace at all. Washington brought his army north, camping in the Hudson Valley near Newburgh, New York. In the cold winter of 1782–1783, Martha sent for a book of psalms so she could bring some Christmas cheer and hope to the headquarters. As winter turned toward spring, Washington began to plan for a possible attack against New York City, in case the British didn't agree to the peace terms and leave on their own.

Meanwhile, the soldiers were still not receiving their money or supplies. Officers began to grumble. In early March of 1783, they passed around a note calling for a meeting on March 11. The letter suggested that the officers desert. It also suggested that, if peace did come, the army shouldn't disband. Instead, it could stay together and force Congress to do what the officers wanted. In other words, the letter proposed a military dictatorship, or control of the country by the military.

Washington had always believed that free men must govern themselves through the rule of law, not through military force. Throughout the war, he deferred to Congress and other elected officials to make political decisions. The letter bothered him a great deal, but a second one alarmed him even further. This contained a more dangerous suggestion. It claimed that General Washington shared the men's complaints, and so he himself might lead the officers to settle their grievances. In other words, having chased King George III's army from America, Washington could make himself dictator, ruler of America.

A very similar suggestion had been made by a man named Lewis Nicola the year before. Nicola believed Washington should in effect be king or emperor of America, and he told him so in a letter. Washington had responded sharply, directing Nicola to "banish these thoughts from your mind." He was not tempted to reconsider now.

Washington ordered that no meeting take place March 11. Instead, there would be one on March 15. He explained privately that he wanted the officers to consider how serious this matter was. At first, he may have intended to send some delegates to the meeting, but he finally decided to attend himself.

"I HAVE GROWN GRAY IN YOUR SERVICE"

No one spoke as he entered the building from the side and made his way to the front. He launched into his speech, expressing his shock at the way they had been called together by an anonymous letter. With all eyes on him in the meeting hall, he told the men that if they went against Congress, they would be going against the people, their own wives and children. "This dreadful alternative, of either deserting our Country in the extremest hour of her distress, or turning our Arms against it . . . has something so shocking in it, that humanity revolts at the idea. My

God! what can this writer [of the letter] have in view, by recommending such measures? Can he be a friend to the Army? Can he be a friend to this Country? Rather, is he not an insidious foe?"

Washington's voice filled the hall as he promised to work to solve their grievances "so far as may be done consistently with the great duty I owe my Country." He noted that Congress had already acted to try and fulfill its promises. And then he roused the officers' patriotism, asking them to "give one more distinguished proof of unexampled patriotism and patient virtue, rising superior to the pressure of the most complicated sufferings."

The speech ended eloquently, but Washington was not quite done. He reached into his pocket and took out a letter from Congress about finances and promises to help the officers. The hall was dark, the writing small. Washington stumbled over a few sentences.

He stopped, and reached into his pocket for his glasses. "Gentlemen," he said as he put them on, "you must pardon me. I have grown gray in your service and now find myself growing blind."

Tears slipped from the eyes of several of the officers. Others turned away to hide their emotion. More than his speech, Washington's own example of personal sacrifice overwhelmed the men. The threat of mutiny, desertion, and military dictatorship evaporated.

FAREWELL

In early September of 1783, the peace treaty between America and Britain was signed. America had won her independence. Parades, fireworks, and festive dinners

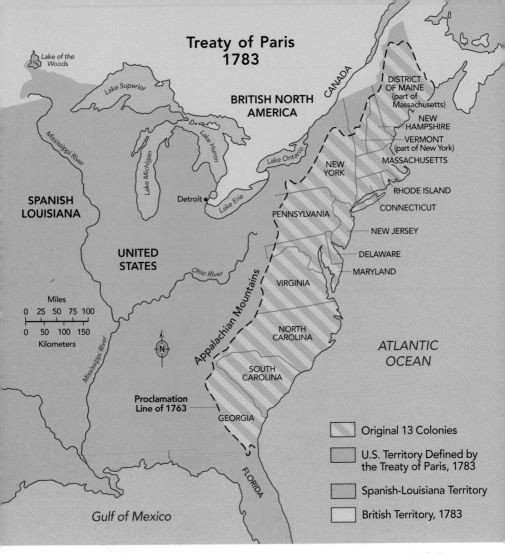

Treaty of Paris 1783

Lake of the Woods

Lake Superior

BRITISH NORTH AMERICA

CANADA

DISTRICT OF MAINE (part of Massachusetts)

NEW HAMPSHIRE

VERMONT (part of New York)

MASSACHUSETTS

Mississippi River

Lake Michigan

Lake Huron

Lake Ontario

NEW YORK

RHODE ISLAND

CONNECTICUT

SPANISH LOUISIANA

Detroit

Lake Erie

PENNSYLVANIA

NEW JERSEY

UNITED STATES

Ohio River

DELAWARE

MARYLAND

VIRGINIA

Miles
0 25 50 75 100

0   50   100   150
Kilometers

Mississippi River

Appalachian Mountains

N

NORTH CAROLINA

ATLANTIC OCEAN

SOUTH CAROLINA

Proclamation Line of 1763

GEORGIA

FLORIDA

Gulf of Mexico

Original 13 Colonies

U.S. Territory Defined by the Treaty of Paris, 1783

Spanish-Louisiana Territory

British Territory, 1783

The 1783 peace agreement between America and Britain was called the Treaty of Paris. It established new boundaries for U.S. territory.

marked the end of the war. The celebrations brought Washington to the outskirts of New York City on November 25 at the head of a large parade of troops and civilians. Many wore the symbols of the Revolution: a ribbon on their jackets and a sprig of laurel in their hats. On December 4, Washington celebrated one last time with some of the officers who had fought with him. In Fraunces Tavern near the southern tip of the city, Washington raised his glass.

"With a heart full of love and gratitude," he said, his voice choked with emotion, "I now take leave of you. I most devoutly wish that your later days may be as prosperous and happy as your former ones have been glorious and honorable."

Late on Christmas Eve, 1783, he rode up the drive to Mount Vernon. There Martha and some of his step-grandchildren hugged him and pulled him inside to the warmth of the fire. Finally, he was home.

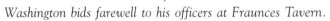

Washington bids farewell to his officers at Fraunces Tavern.

CHAPTER 6

A MORE PERFECT UNION

"Agriculture has ever been amongst the most favorite amusements of my life, though I never possessed much skill in the art."
—George Washington to a friend in 1786

There were shapes and voices outside. An angel—or maybe a devil—prodded Washington to wake up from his slumber. Work to be done! An army to feed and clothe! The enemy was marching from New York, determined to kill his men and drag him back to London in chains!

Washington woke with a start. He was in his bed, safe in Mount Vernon. His wife and servants were all asleep. The war was over. It was just another of his dreams. He went back to sleep.

A few hours later, refreshed, Washington rose and began his morning routine. There was much to do at Mount Vernon. The plantation was its own little village. There was always activity and work to be done. Besides the main house and the many acres of farmland, the plantation had outbuildings such as servants' quarters and a kitchen. It had barns and other farm buildings such as a dung house and a smith's forge. It even had a kennel that housed seven French foxhounds. Besides running the farm, Washington was championing a plan to build a canal in the interior of the country.

In the years after the war, Washington spent many of his mornings making the rounds of his farm. Often there would be visitors waiting when he returned to the house. Officers from the war and friends such as Thomas Jefferson, James Madison, and other Virginia politicians often came by. Countless people Washington didn't know also stopped to meet the famous general. As Washington said in a letter, "scarcely any strangers who are going from North to South, or from South to North, do not spend a day or two."

Washington and his guests would eat dinner between two and three. He would then leave them to spend the afternoon in his library or his gardens. He was usually in bed by nine o'clock—although with some friends he stayed up late to chat, to drink "several glasses of champagne and get 'quite merry.'" The Washingtons sometimes held large parties and dances in their home. They even added a new banquet hall for these occasions.

The Washingtons did not have children together, and by this time, Martha's children had all died. Her son Jackie left her four grandchildren. The two youngest, Eleanor or "Nellie" (age four at the end of the war) and George Washington Parke Custis or "Tub" (age two), were raised at Mount Vernon. Washington loved and indulged his step-grandchildren.

*Washington talks with Martha and her young grandchildren
on the porch of Mount Vernon.*

———————————— ✧ ————————————

Washington and Martha remained a devoted couple. "I
have always considered marriage as the most interesting
event of one's life," wrote Washington, "the foundation of
happiness or misery." For him, it was happiness. But by late
1786, worries about his country began intruding into the
joy he had found at Mount Vernon.

ARTICLES OF CONFEDERATION
The states and Congress had spent several years during the
war trying to decide what shape and powers the national
government should have. Their deliberations produced the
Articles of Confederation. It was finally ratified, or
approved, in 1781. The Articles of Confederation outlined a
government that gave the Continental Congress control over
foreign affairs and the military. But it had no authority over

the states. Even before the Articles of Confederation were ratified, many leaders argued that the country needed a stronger central government. For one thing, the war left the country with large debts that would be easier for a central government to pay off. A strong national government could encourage trade and improve the economy. The government could also balance the interests of different classes in America.

In the fall of 1786, a group of farmers took up arms in Massachusetts. In what became known as Shays's Rebellion, they vowed to "annihilate all debts public and private" and make all property "common property of all." Washington, like many others, saw the revolt as a sign that chaos was growing. His friend Benjamin Lincoln, a general who had served under Washington, ended the rebellion by marching the state militia against the mob. But the possibility of chaos remained, not just in Massachusetts but throughout the country. Like many others, Washington came to feel that only a strong national government could guarantee order. He joined other political leaders in urging that a convention be held to discuss a new government.

Even so Washington was not sure that he should attend the convention himself. He wanted to remain retired from public life. Historians also think he was worried about damaging his reputation by becoming involved in the debates and political squabbles that were sure to follow. In a letter to Henry Knox, another of his former generals, on February 3, 1787, Washington said "it is not, at this time, my purpose to attend [the convention]." But a month later, he wrote to Knox, "A thought . . . has lately run through my mind, which is attended with embarrassment."

Washington had begun to believe that it was his duty to attend. He had fought hard to make America a democracy during the Revolution. This was a new fight for the same cause. His country needed him again, and he could not refuse.

NEW CONSTITUTION

On May 14, 1787, Washington strode into a room he knew well—the assembly room at the State House in Philadelphia. Chairs scraped as the few men already there rose quickly to greet him.

But the convention could not begin. Only two states had delegates there, Virginia and Pennsylvania. Delegates from at least seven states were needed for work to begin. Washington, who always valued punctuality, felt disgusted. But he and the others could only wait as delegates from the other states slowly made their way to Philadelphia.

Washington put the time to good use. He and other Virginians had helped fellow Virginian James Madison refine a far-reaching plan for a new government. Madison's blueprint, which would be called the Virginia Plan, radically reorganized the government. As delegates made their way into the city, Washington talked to them and drummed up support for the plan.

In some ways, the Constitutional Convention was a series of debates over governmental theory. At most sessions, somewhere between twenty and thirty delegates would discuss different matters in detail. Unanimously elected to chair the convention, Washington sat at the front of the room during every formal session. His role was mostly to encourage discussion—and to keep debates from

James Madison (left) and Alexander Hamilton (right) worked together to convince the states to approve the Constitution.

getting out of hand. He gave only one speech, although other delegates undoubtedly considered his private opinions extremely important. When the work was over in mid-September, the new Constitution was presented to the states for ratification.

"The constitution that is submitted, is not free from imperfections," Washington wrote to his friend and aide David Humphreys after returning to Mount Vernon in October of 1787. "But there are as few radical defects in it as could well be expected.... I think it would be wise in the People to adopt what is offered to them."

Madison and Alexander Hamilton, among many others, took a much greater role than Washington did in the campaign to adopt the new Constitution. His support, however, was obvious and important. On several occasions, he urged other prominent Americans to back the plan. Finally, in June of 1788, New Hampshire became the ninth state to ratify the Constitution, establishing it as the law of the land.

A RELUCTANT PRESIDENT

The Constitution divided government into three branches—
the executive, judicial, and legislative. The legislative branch
(Congress) passed laws. Congress was divided into two
sections, the Senate and the House of Representatives. The
judicial branch provided courts where legal issues could be
heard. The executive branch, led by a president, carried out
the laws. The president also led the army.

Historians believe that Washington was one reason
many of the authors of the Constitution gave the executive
branch a great deal of power. Even before the Constitution
was adopted, most people thought he would be America's
first president.

Except Washington didn't want the job. In his mid-
fifties by this time, Washington had reached what was then
considered old age. While still in good health overall, his
eyesight and hearing were not as good as they once had
been. He also had serious trouble with his teeth, which no
set of false teeth could fix.

Washington knew that leading the country would be a
grueling job. The government outlined by the Constitution
was an enormous experiment. There were as many reasons
why it could fail as succeed. From a modern-day perspec-
tive, it seems impossible to separate the idea of democracy
from the United States. But at the time, both were new,
radical concepts.

Washington also worried that the job would hurt his
reputation, which he valued more than his property. Some
people were bound to dislike things he did. On the other
hand, he had a strong sense of duty. And he worried about
what would happen to the country if he didn't take the job.

In a private letter, Washington told the Marquis de Lafayette (the Frenchman who had fought along with Washington) that the presidency "has no enticing charms, and no [attractions] for me. . . . The growing love of retirement do[es] not permit me to entertain a wish beyond that of living and dying an honest man on my own farm. Let those follow the pursuits of ambition and fame, who have a keener relish for them, or who may have more years, in store, for the enjoyment." When Washington's friend

MYTHS

Many myths have been created about George Washington. Though they are made up, they often show a real part of his personality. Probably the most famous tale is about a cherry tree. According to the story, young Washington was playing and decided to chop down his father's cherry tree. His father saw the ruined tree and asked him what had happened. Washington replied, "I cannot tell a lie. I chopped down the cherry tree."

This story tells readers that Washington was so honest, he could not lie even when faced with punishment. It was invented by an early biographer who wanted to show that Washington was a very honest general and politician.

One popular story about George Washington is true—he did have false teeth. In the age before modern dentistry, tooth and gum problems were common. He tried many different sets of false teeth during his life but never found a set that was comfortable or long lasting. The materials used to make his false teeth ranged from wood to hippopotamus tusk.

Benjamin Lincoln tried to persuade him to run for election, he told him that he did not want to.

But by the beginning of 1789, Washington apparently decided he had no choice. He drew up instructions for running the farm in his absence. In the meantime, the states began selecting presidential electors (the group of people who would elect the president), as directed by the Constitution. When the electors met on February 4, 1789, their decision was unanimous. George Washington was selected to serve as the first president of the United States of America. As he waited for the Senate to meet and confirm the election as provided by the Constitution, Washington wrapped up his business and personal affairs. Among other things, he visited his eighty-year-old mother, who was slowly dying of breast cancer. He strongly suspected it would be the last time he would see her alive.

On April 14, the secretary of Congress arrived at Mount Vernon to inform Washington officially that he had been elected president. In his empty dining room, Washington accepted the summons. "I bade adieu to Mount Vernon, to private life, and to domestic [joy], and with a mind oppressed with more anxious and painful sensations than I have words to express, set out for New York," Washington told his journal as he started the trip to New York City, the country's temporary capital.

CHAPTER 7

INVENTING GOVERNMENT

"No People can be bound to acknowledge
and adore the invisible hand, which conducts
the Affairs of men more than the People
of the United States."
—George Washington's First Inaugural Address, 1789

George Washington stood in the light spring breeze as twenty-six men propelled his barge through New York Harbor to the wharf at the foot of Wall Street. Boats and ships of all kinds floated in the river around him. As he reached the shore, the crowd roared. As Washington began walking the few blocks to his rented house on Cherry Street in the country's new capital of New York City, the crowd surged around him. It seemed to take forever to walk the half mile to his new home. No other president would ever receive such adoration upon taking office. In fact, Washington himself would never again enjoy such adoration from so many different people.

Washington takes the presidential oath of office in New York City on April 30, 1789.

✧ ————————

THE EXPERIMENT OF GOVERNMENT

When Washington was inaugurated president a week later, he told Congress that the new government had to work hard to preserve "the experiment entrusted to the hands of the American people." Among the problems facing the government were large debts, the need for better transportation, and the lack of industries. Washington urged everyone in Congress to work together.

Besides dealing with the problems facing America, Washington had to invent what is known in modern times as the "image," or social aspects, of a president. Kings used several methods to show their importance and to give their government an air of authority. How should a president do that? By acting like a king? What should he wear? How should he be introduced at public gatherings?

Washington tried to balance democratic practices with more stately ones. For example, he wanted to let anyone in the country visit him. But to keep from being overrun, he had to establish a schedule of meetings. That was not simple. At one of his first levees, or open meetings, Washington's assistant David Humphreys threw open the doors in front of him and shouted, "The president of the United States!" According to Thomas Jefferson, Washington was so embarrassed at being announced like a king that he told Humphreys, "Well you have taken me in once, but by God, you shall never take me in a second time!" His solution was simple: he made sure he was already in the room when guests came in so he didn't have to be introduced.

Martha joined Washington at the capital as First Lady. She soon earned a reputation as a gracious host, though the need to entertain many visitors caused the Washingtons to overspend their budget. In his second year in office, Washington overspent his $25,000 salary by about $7,000.

Washington's parties were attended by many important members of the government as well as by his old friends. He even entertained enemies. When Senator William Maclay—a staunch opponent of Washington and a man one historian called a "grouch"—came to dinner, Washington treated him warmly. Maclay finally had to admit Washington had "a good nature."

On September 1, 1789, Washington joined Revolutionary War general von Steuben and some other friends for dinner. As they laughed over dinner, a message came that Washington's mother had died on July 25. "Awful, and affecting as the death of a parent is, there is consolation in knowing that Heaven has spared ours to an age, beyond which few attain," Washington wrote his sister Betty two weeks later.

A STAR-STUDDED CABINET

To help him deal with the problems of the country, Washington chose a number of secretaries, or department heads, to advise him and to handle different governmental duties. This group eventually came to be called the cabinet. Washington's appointees included people who are considered some of the most important Americans ever to serve the government. Thomas Jefferson became secretary of state. His primary job was helping Washington deal with foreign governments. Alexander Hamilton, Washington's former aide and a New York politician, became secretary of the treasury. The treasury was in charge of collecting taxes and paying bills and debts. General Knox headed the war department, which oversaw the army. Other notable Americans in government included Vice President John Adams, one of the leaders of the Revolution; John Jay, chief justice of the Supreme Court; and Madison, who became a leader in the House of Representatives.

One of the most important problems the country

✧ ————————————

Members of Washington's cabinet included (from left to right): Knox, Jefferson, Hamilton, and Attorney General Edmund Randolph.

faced was paying off the debt from the Revolution. Hamilton estimated that the government owed approximately $40 million to Americans (many of them soldiers) and more than $10 million to foreigners. His solution came in three parts. Congress easily accepted the first part, to replace some of this debt with bonds. These bonds were a type of loan to the government. They would be paid back a little at a time with tax money. The plan also helped the economy by keeping money circulating.

Two other parts of his plan were very controversial and stirred the first great debates of Washington's administration. During the Revolution, soldiers and farmers were paid with certificates promising full payment in the future. In many cases, the people who received these certificates had sold them to others in order to have money to live on. These sales were often at a fraction of the value of the original certificate. Hamilton wanted to pay off all of these certificates at their full value. The plan greatly benefited speculators and merchants who had been well off enough to buy the certificates at low prices. Critics said Hamilton favored the rich over the patriotic but poor soldiers.

Hamilton also wanted the federal government to assume state debts from the war. Some states had not paid off these loans, while others already had. Those states that had were opposed to the idea.

The debate over the country's debts was not just about money. It was about how the government should serve people of different classes and people in different regions. Ultimately, deciding how to pay off the debts and raise taxes involved an even larger question. Should the country primarily be one of farmers or of merchants and businessmen? In other words, who should benefit most from the laws the government made?

Washington did not get directly involved in the debate, which eventually split his advisers as well as Congress. Historians believe that he generally backed Hamilton's plans, though there is not a great deal of evidence. In the end, he agreed with a complicated compromise that Jefferson helped engineer. The plan not only settled the debt question largely as Hamilton had proposed but also chose the Potomac River area as the permanent site for the United States capital. Washington favored the site and so did Jefferson and other Virginia politicians.

The new president attempted to stand above political arguments. He seemed content to have the Congress debate and compromise and then present him with a bill to sign into law. Even so, he was criticized. A Boston paper suggested he had betrayed his promises to his troops by accepting Hamilton's repayment plan.

IMPLIED POWERS

Finances began to divide the country's politicians more and more. In 1790 Hamilton made two more proposals that were extremely controversial. The first was for a tax on liquor, such as whiskey. The second would create a Bank of the United States. This bank, partly owned by the government, would be able to issue currency, or money. In many respects, it was modeled after the highly successful Bank of England.

Though there were some objections, the whiskey tax was easily passed. The Senate voted to create the bank as well. But when the House of Representatives met to vote on the measure, Madison rose to oppose it. He pointed out that the Constitution did not state that Congress could create a bank.

The House voted in favor of the law, 39 to 20. But Madison's opposition troubled Washington deeply. Besides being his friend, Madison was the main author of the Constitution and knew more about it than anyone. Was Congress acting illegally? How much power did it really have?

Others who had been at the Constitutional Convention disagreed with Madison's interpretation. They said that Congress had what are known as "implied powers." In other words, Congress could choose how to reach the general goals the Constitution set out. It could do this as long as those means were not specifically forbidden.

Washington and Madison discussed the issue several times in "free conversations." Washington asked both Jefferson and Attorney General Edmund Randolph for their opinions. Both declared the law unconstitutional.

Hamilton disagreed. He prepared a fifteen-thousand-word response arguing that the federal government had the right to take reasonable steps to carry out its duties. If creating a bank was necessary to regulate the economy, then Congress could do so.

—————————— ✧

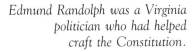

Edmund Randolph was a Virginia politician who had helped craft the Constitution.

Washington weighed all the arguments for several days. Finally, he decided to sign the bill into law. His decision firmly established the idea of implied powers.

TWO PARTIES

The debates over financial issues caused a split in Washington's cabinet. This mirrored a similar split in Congress. The two groups, known as the Federalists and the Republicans, soon became two political parties.

Federalists believed in a very powerful federal government. Federalists favored laws and measures that benefited businesses such as trade, banking, and manufacturing. Hamilton was among their leaders, but many others, including John Adams, would play important roles when the party was formally established a few years later.

The Republicans—also called the Republican-Democrats and simply Democrats—had a different vision. They emphasized the needs of ordinary white citizens. Their policies and laws tended to favor farmers and rural areas. Republicans in general were very suspicious of a strong central government, though they recognized it was important to protect individual rights. Jefferson and Madison were among their leaders. (Though first known as the Republican Party, the party actually became the modern Democratic Party.)

As time went on, Jefferson and Hamilton became personal enemies. The animosity between them was hard on Washington, who continued to work with them both.

Washington continued to oppose all political parties. He tried not to favor the interests of particular groups or regions. Still, historians say that as time went on, his political philosophy as president was closer to that of the Federalists.

By the end of his presidency, Federalists dominated his cabinet, despite Washington's efforts to keep it balanced.

FRANCE

On July 28, 1791, Washington sat at his desk in the new capital, Philadelphia, and began a letter to his friend the Marquis de Lafayette. He had recently received a report from Lafayette of events in France and was deeply troubled.

"I have often contemplated, with great anxiety, the danger to which you are personally exposed," Washington told his friend, gently warning him not to be too brave. France was in the middle of its own revolution. When the French Revolution began in 1789, it seemed in some ways an echo of the American Revolution. The aim of many French people, including Lafayette, was to establish a representative government. But chaos had grown, especially in cities such as Paris. When the king left Paris, a mob took him prisoner. Massacres, terror, chaos, and eventually war would follow.

───────────────── ✧ ─────────────────

On July 14, 1789, an angry mob attacked the Bastille, a Paris fortress used as a prison. The storming of the Bastille marked the beginning of the French Revolution.

When he wrote to Lafayette, Washington did not know that the king had tried to flee. But he warned against "the tumultuous populace of large cities"—mobs which could get out of control. On the same day, he wrote to the American representative in Paris, Gouverneur Morris, and said that democracy in France was a good thing. But he also warned that America must carefully consider "connexions" with "any European power." He was thinking of the growing conflict between France and Great Britain. While Washington's policies seemed initially to favor France, he wanted America to stay neutral.

About a month later, Jefferson told Washington that the mob had turned against the king. Washington seemed "devastated." He concluded that the French Revolution had spun out of control. At the same time, the increasing conflict between France and Great Britain aggravated the differences between the two different factions in American government. The Republicans wanted America to ally itself with France. The Federalists wanted either neutrality or closer ties with Great Britain.

Conflicts in Europe and political scrapes were not Washington's only concern as his presidential term continued. In December 1791, a letter arrived from the frontier informing him that the troops he had sent to quell Indian attacks in the area that is now Fort Wayne, Indiana, had suffered a terrible defeat. In all, more than nine hundred U.S. soldiers had been killed or wounded. Washington, who had warned the commander to be on his guard, flew into a rage at the news. When he calmed, he sent a new force west. This force succeeded in defeating the warring Indians.

As the end of his term approached, Washington thought about retirement once more. He badly wanted to go home to Mount Vernon. So did Martha. He was tired and frustrated. Many people had begun to criticize him. Some charged that he was pushing America toward monarchy. Jefferson, though he wanted Washington to remain president, had hired an editor to publish a newspaper that continually attacked Hamilton's views—and Washington himself. "I shall be happy... to see a cessation of the abuses," Washington wrote Edmund Randolph, saying that he looked forward to the end of the criticism. He worried that the attacks would hurt the country.

Still, both the Federalists and Republicans urged him not to retire. Washington seemed the only man in America who could work with both sides. The growing possibility of war in Europe, as well as problems in America, finally convinced Washington that he had to remain as president. But he wrote to Henry Lee in January 1793, after his reelection, stating that "to say I feel pleasure from the prospect of commencing another tour of duty would be a departure from the truth."

CHAPTER 8

PROBLEMS AND MORE PROBLEMS

"Truth or falsehood is immaterial to them,
provided their objects are promoted."
—George Washington, writing to his friend
Henry Lee, about his political enemies

The carriage bumped to a stop at the center of Carlisle, a small town in western Pennsylvania near the Allegheny Mountains. The sixty-two-year-old Washington rose from his seat and got out slowly, feeling old and tired. The president had known the frontier as a young man, protecting it during the French and Indian War. The area had prospered greatly since then. Riding on the road to Carlisle, he had admired the fields rich with their late summer crops.

But he had not traveled here to inspect his country's prosperity. He had come because many of the farmers beyond the mountain pass ahead had taken up arms against the law, refusing to pay the tax on whiskey. A tax collector's home had been burned, and more violence was threatened. Washington feared that if such troubles continued, chaos and even civil war might threaten the entire country. He had called out the militia in four nearby states, placing them under his command. He thought a show of force would make the farmers obey the law without bloodshed. He hoped to take care of matters quickly and then head down to Mount Vernon for badly needed rest.

But as he got out of the carriage, the president saw how ragged and unorganized the militiamen were. He wouldn't be able to head home any time soon. Washington went to work training the group.

Soon after his arrival, two men arrived in town and asked to speak to him. The men claimed that the rebellion had been started by a small group of radicals who were opposed not just to the tax but "to all law and government." The people in the area were shocked to find out that the government intended on enforcing the law with troops. They had thought everyone in the country was opposed to the tax and therefore the government would not bother to collect it.

———————————————— ✧ ————————————————

Western Pennsylvania farmers threaten local tax collectors.

Washington set them straight. The tax was law. Popular or not, it would be collected. The rebellion quickly collapsed.

WHISKEY AND OTHER CONCERNS

The Whiskey Rebellion was the most serious challenge to the government since Shays's Rebellion (the Massachusetts farmers' revolt that had helped inspire the new Constitution). Washington's presence calmed and controlled the situation. While he was firm with the rebels, he also prevented them from being "skewered, hanged or shot in cold blood" by the militia, as one of the negotiators put it.

Washington's actions set yet another precedent for a strong central government. Even unpopular laws would be enforced. He also made it clear that the expanding western fringes of the country were a part of the United States.

But the Whiskey Rebellion increased friction between the Federalists and the Republicans. And when Washington criticized citizen groups for encouraging revolt, Republican leaders said he was being antidemocratic. Washington, who considered the criticism unfair, was deeply hurt by the attacks on his character and principles.

Despite the growing conflicts at the capital and the looming war in Europe, Washington was able to find time for more pleasant concerns. The president oversaw some of the early planning for the new capital city. He also made provisions for a college there. The president even found time to offer his step-granddaughter Nellie advice on marriage. "When the fire is beginning to kindle, and your heart growing warm, propound [pose] these questions to it. Who is this invader? Have I a competent knowledge of him? Is he a man of good character; a man of sense?"

BETRAYAL

When Jefferson resigned his post in 1793, Edmund Randolph replaced him as secretary of state. Washington considered him a friend and often consulted with him in private on a variety of matters besides foreign affairs.

When France and Great Britain finally went to war, Washington continued to maintain America's neutrality. He sent John Jay to negotiate a new treaty with Britain. When he read a draft of the treaty in late 1793, Washington felt it was far from perfect. It did provide for the British to withdraw from forts on the American frontier, which was one of Washington's main goals. And it allowed free navigation on the Mississippi River, another important point.

On the other hand, it did not prevent American sailors from being taken from ships and forced to join the British navy. And the terms it set out for trade in the West Indies were also considered unfavorable to the Americans.

Washington debated what to do. Should he tear up the treaty and start from scratch? Or should he accept it as the best possible compromise? Finally, he decided to go ahead and present the treaty to the Senate. The Senate ratified it, with reservations, in a close vote the following year. But Randolph advised Washington to delay signing it so he could have it changed in the manner the Senate wanted. Washington agreed.

Soon after, two other cabinet members presented Washington with documents that showed Randolph might have been bribed by the French to delay the treaty. This was a betrayal of his country and, also important, Randolph's friendship with the president. Washington signed the treaty and then began considering what to do about his friend.

CONFRONTATION

Washington rose as Randolph walked into the room. It was August 19, 1794, a warm and muggy day in Philadelphia. The secretary of state started to apologize for having been delayed, but the president stopped him with his most formal manner. He told him to sit near Secretary of War Timothy Pickering and Secretary of the Treasury Oliver Wolcott. Surprised at the formality, Randolph sat.

"Mr. Randolph," said Washington, reaching into his pocket and pulling out a bundle of papers, "here is a letter which I desire you to read, and make such explanations as you choose." Washington carefully studied Randolph's manner. The evidence was not overwhelming, and Washington had decided he would judge his friend's guilt or innocence from his reaction. At first, the president was pleased that Randolph said he was innocent. But when Randolph became excited and agitated, Washington believed this meant he was guilty.

Historians think Randolph did not accept a bribe. But Washington believed that he could assess a man's character by watching his reactions. The president judged Randolph by the high standards that he set for himself. When his emotions made it seem that he did not meet those standards, the president felt deeply betrayed. Randolph quickly resigned.

EXECUTIVE PRIVILEGE

The controversy over Jay's Treaty led to further fights, including one between Washington and the House of Representatives the following year. The House demanded papers from Washington that showed exactly what instructions he had given Jay during the negotiations. Washington sent a message back to Congress saying he would not comply: "To admit . . . a right in the House of Representative to demand, and to have as a matter of course, all the Papers respecting a negotiation with a foreign power, would be to establish a dangerous precedent."

Washington did not want to turn over the papers for several reasons. One was probably that he didn't want to be embarrassed or second-guessed by the congressmen. But there were also more important issues at stake. If a president had to turn over all of his papers regarding negotiations, he would never be able to keep negotiations secret. That might hurt his ability to negotiate in the future. Even more importantly, if Congress could order the president to do something, this implied that Congress was more important than the president. Giving in to a demand not outlined in the Constitution would compromise the president's role in government.

Washington's answer firmly established the power and independence of the executive branch. And "executive privilege"—the ability of the president to keep his papers secret—became an important part of American government.

FAREWELL
On September 19, 1796, a long notice appeared on the front page of the *American Daily Advertiser* in Philadelphia. It began, "Friends, and Fellow-Citizens: The period for a new election of a Citizen, to Administer the Executive government of the United States, being not far distant . . . I should now apprise you of the resolution I have formed, to decline being considered among the number of those, out of whom a choice is to be made." Washington was telling the country he was retiring.

SLAVERY

Like many other Americans, Washington owned slaves for most of his life. But as he grew older, he grew less and less comfortable with the idea of slavery.

In 1786 there were 216 slaves at Mount Vernon. About half were Washington's. The others belonged to the Custis family. By then his feelings toward slavery were changing. He seems to have gradually begun to regret having slaves at all. In 1788 or 1789, he told David Humphreys, "The unfortunate condition of the persons, whose labor in part I employed, has been the only unavoidable subject of regret."

When Washington left the presidency in 1797, he took advantage of a Pennsylvania state law to free some of his slaves. According to the state law, they would be freed simply by being in the state for six months after their owner became a state resident. Washington let them remain long enough for them to gain their freedom legally. His will, written two years later, freed all the slaves he owned. It also stated that his heirs should care for those slaves who were too young or too old to care for themselves. Those not freed immediately were "to be taught to read and write; and to be brought up to some useful occupation."

On the other hand, Washington did not use his prestige to fight against slavery. Nor did he demonstrate his second thoughts on slavery with bold actions during his lifetime. He did not, for example, urge that laws be passed to abolish it or free all of his slaves openly. "Slavery, in his eyes, was a wasteful nuisance," declared biographer Freeman, "but so long as it existed in a country where the sentiment of honest men was divided over it, he would safeguard his rights with the least public offense."

Unlike in modern times, in 1796 there were no limits as to how long a person could serve as president. Despite the personal attacks on him, Washington was still adored by most and could easily have won reelection.

The notice in the newspaper spoke of many things Washington had long been concerned about. He stressed that the entire country must work together in government, and he emphasized the wisdom of staying out of European wars. As far as Washington was concerned, however, the most important thing the notice said was simply that he would no longer serve as president. It was time to rest.

MOUNT VERNON

After he left the capital and returned to Mount Vernon in 1797, many visitors stopped by to see the famous general and retired president. Washington spent much of his time and energy running the plantation. He organized his collection of paintings, which included American natural landscapes. He also tried to increase his income by speculating in more land. He had been unable to save any of his income while in office and had many bills to pay.

Washington was relieved to spend his time quietly at Mount Vernon after his terms as president.

But Washington was not through with public life altogether. About a year after he left office, relations between America and France reached a boiling point. Washington offered to help President John Adams lead the army in case of war. Adams appointed him lieutenant general and commander of all military forces. Washington quickly became embroiled in disagreements over who should be his second in command. He eventually got his way, appointing his old friend and former aide, Hamilton, but only after threatening to resign.

Historians point out that his letters and conduct show that Washington had lost the composure and judgment that had once been the cornerstone of his character. "At various moments in the controversy," writes biographer Flexner, "the brilliant pragmatist seems to have lost touch with reality."

At sixty-six, Washington was past his prime, and he probably recognized this himself. He fended off suggestions that he run for election in the next presidential race, scheduled for 1800.

"I DIE HARD"

It snowed hard the morning of December 13, 1799. Sometime during the day, George Washington began feeling a scratch in his throat. He and Martha sat down in the parlor with his secretary Tobias Lear late in the day, reading newspapers. The general laughed and seemed in good spirits, but his sore throat kept getting worse.

After he and his wife went to bed, he woke Martha to tell her that he felt terrible. His throat ached, and he had trouble breathing. But then he wouldn't let her get up to

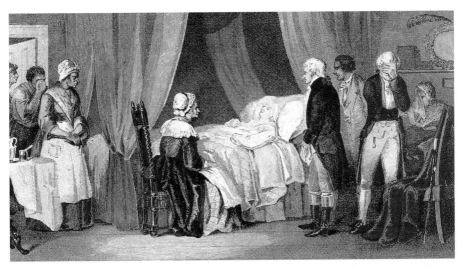

Washington died surrounded by his family and devoted friends.

tend to him. The house was so cold, he didn't want her catching a chill.

By the next afternoon, December 14, Washington realized he wasn't going to get better. "I die hard, but I am not afraid to go," he told his doctor. Modern physicians have been unable to decide precisely what disease Washington had. The doctors of the time diagnosed it as tonsillitis but lacked medicine to cure it.

Some of Washington's friends and family, including Martha and Lear, gathered at his bedside. Near midnight Washington moved his hand to his arm and took his pulse. Then the general's hand slipped to the side, limp. He had passed away into history.

TIMELINE

1732 Washington is born on February 22 to Mary Ball and Augustine "Gus" Washington.

1739 Washington begins his education.

1743 Augustine Washington, Washington's father, dies. Washington's half-brother Lawrence inherits most of his property. Lawrence marries Anne Fairfax, a member of the important Fairfax family.

1747 Washington begins to study surveying.

1748 Washington goes on a surveying trip in the Shenandoah Valley. After that he makes many more surveying trips.

1751 Washington accompanies Lawrence to Barbados to seek a cure for Lawrence's tuberculosis.

1752 Lawrence dies in July. In November Washington is appointed a major in the colonial militia.

1754 Washington leads a small force that surprises a group of French soldiers, killing a French diplomat. In July Colonel Washington suffers an embarrassing defeat when his troops are beaten at Fort Necessity.

1755 Washington serves in the French and Indian War (1754–1763) with British General Edward Braddock.

1759 Washington marries Martha Dandridge Custis. He devotes himself to improving Mount Vernon, their plantation.

1769 Emotions in America grow against the British Parliament as many colonists protest the Townshend Acts.

1774 Following the Boston Tea Party in December 1773, Washington is selected to attend the First Continental Congress.

1775 The Revolutionary War erupts. Washington attends the Second Continental Congress and is selected commander in chief of the army.

1776 The Declaration of Independence is written. On December 26, Washington captures nine hundred prisoners at Trenton, his first great victory of the war.

1780 Washington is betrayed by General Benedict Arnold.

1781 The states adopt the Articles of Confederation. Washington leads the army to Yorktown and defeats Cornwallis in October. This is the last major battle of the Revolutionary War.

1783 Britain and America sign a peace treaty.

1784–1787 Washington returns to Mount Vernon. He works to restore all of his business interests.

1787 Washington presides at the Constitutional Convention in Philadelphia.

1788 The ninth state (New Hampshire) ratifies the Constitution, making it the law of the land.

1789 Washington is elected president.

1792 Political splits grow in Congress and the country. Leading politicians convince Washington to run for a second term as president. He is reelected in December.

1794 Acting as commander of several militias, President Washington suppresses the Whiskey Rebellion.

1796 Washington decides he will not run for reelection and has his decision published.

1797 Washington retires to Mount Vernon.

1799 Washington dies the night of December 14.

SOURCE NOTES

7 George Washington, *George Washington Writings*, ed. John Rhodehamel (New York: The Library of America, 1997), 1018.

9 Ibid., 7. (In most cases where original documents are used in this book, the spelling has been modernized for convenience.)

12 Ibid., 3. (Spelling and punctuation are from the original.) The exact date that Washington wrote the rules is unknown, but it was before he reached his teens, probably between ten and twelve.

13 Ibid.

14 James Thomas Flexner, *George Washington: The Forge of Experience (1732–1775)* (Boston: Little, Brown and Company, 1965), 19.

14 Washington, *Writings*, 50.

17 Ibid., 12.

23 Ibid., 60.

24 Flexner, *Forge of Experience*, 75. Flexner's source for the incident are journals kept by Gist.

25 Ibid., 81–82, quoting from Dinwiddie's earlier orders, still in effect.

26 Washington, *Writings*, 48. The number of prisoners in Washington's letter differs with the numbers generally given by historians.

33 Ibid., 99.

34 Ibid., 160.

37 Flexner, *Forge of Experience*, 251.

38 Ibid., 272.

39 Ibid., 289.

40 Washington, *Writings*, 114.

41 Ibid., 130.

42 Douglas Southall Freeman, *George Washington, A Biography*, vol. 3 (New York: Charles Scribner's Sons, 1951), 350.

42 Paul K. Longmore, *The Invention of George Washington* (Charlottesville: University Press of Virginia, 1999), 113. He is quoting from a letter to George William Fairfax.

45 Washington, *Writings*, 167.

45 Ibid., 168.

45 Ibid., 169.

47 Ibid., 305.

51 Washington, *Writings*, 241.

54 Freeman, *Washington*, vol. 3, 193. This story is repeated in countless places.

54 Robert Leckie, *George Washington's War*, (New York: HarperCollins, 1992), 277. There is some question over Washington's exact words, but his anger is attested to by many who were there.

55 Freeman, *Washington*, vol. 3, 202.

55 Ibid., 207.

55 James Thomas Flexner, *George Washington in the American Revolution (1775–1783)* (Boston: Little, Brown and Company, 1968), 412.

55 Ibid., 412–413.

56 Joseph Plumb Martin, *Private Yankee Doodle*, (1830; reprint, Washington, D.C.: Eastern Acorn Press, 1993), 284.

56 Ibid., 284.

57 Ibid., 236.

58 Richard M. Ketchum, *The Winter Soldiers*, (1973; reprint, New York: Owl Books, 1999), 253.

59 Washington, *Writings*, 262.

61 John E. Ferling, *The First of Men* (Knoxville: The University of Tennessee Press, 1988), 222. Ferling is specifically referring here to Valley Forge, but the comments apply to the entire war.

63 Washington, *Writings*, 490.
64 Ibid, 407.
65 Ibid., 413.
65 Flexner, *George Washington in the American Revolution*, 409.
65 Leckie, *George Washington's War*, 631.
66 Ibid., 657.
68 Washington, *Writings*, 469.
68–69 Washington, *Writings*, 496–500.
69 Douglas Southall Freeman, *George Washington, A Biography*, vol. 5 (New York: Charles Scribner's Sons, 1952), 435. Freeman points out some of the quibbles historians have raised about the exact words Washington used and the letter he read from in a note at the bottom of the page.
71 Ibid., 467.
72 Washington, *Writings*, 602.
73 Douglas Southall Freeman, *George Washington, A Biography*, vol. 6 (New York: Charles Scribner's Sons, 1954), 159.
73 James Thomas Flexner, *George Washington and the New Nation (1783–1793)*, (Boston: Little, Brown and Company, 1970), 23.
74 Ibid., 36.
75 Ibid., 98.
75 Washington, *Writings*, 634.
76 Ibid., 642.
77 Ibid., 657.
79 Ibid., 679–680.
80 Ibid., 730.
81 Ibid., 731.
82 Ibid., 733.
83 Flexner, *Washington and the New Nation*, 197.
83 Ibid., 283.
83 Ibid., 284.
83 Washington, *Writings*, 740.
87 Robert A. Rutland, *James Madison:*

The Founding Father (New York: Macmillan Publishing Company, 1987), 98.
89 Washington, *Writings*, 780.
90 Ibid.
90 Ibid., 782.
90 Flexner, *Washington and the New Nation*, 293.
91 Washington, *Writings*, 821.
91 Ibid., 833.
92 Ibid., 876.
93 James Thomas Flexner, *George Washington: Anguish and Farewell (1793–1799)* (Boston: Little, Brown and Company, 1972), 174. Flexner is quoting from Washington's diary on the incident. The details there are confirmed by one of the negotiators in a separate account.
94 Ibid, p. 175.
94 Washington, *Writings*, 902.
96 Flexner, *Anguish and Farewell*, 175.
97 Ibid., 931.
97 Ibid., 962.
98 Washington, *Writings*, 702.
98 Ibid., 1023.
98 Freeman, *Washington*, vol. 6, 309.
100 Flexner, *Anguish and Farewell*, 411.
101 Ibid., 460.

BIBLIOGRAPHY

Alden, John R. *George Washington*. Baton Rouge: Louisiana State University Press, 1984.

Baldwin, Leland D. *Whiskey Rebels*. Pittsburgh: University of Pittsburgh Press, 1968.

Billias, George Athan, ed. *George Washington's Generals and Opponents*. New York: DaCapo Press, 1994.

Brookhiser, Richard. *Alexander Hamilton, American*. New York: The Free Press, 1999.

————. *Founding Father: Rediscovering George Washington*. New York: The Free Press, 1996.

Davis, Burke. *George Washington and the American Revolution*. New York: Random House, 1975.

Ferling, John E. *The First of Men*. Knoxville: University of Tennessee Press, 1988.

Flexner, James Thomas. *George Washington in the American Revolution (1775–1783)*. Boston: Little, Brown and Company, 1968.

————. *George Washington: Anguish and Farewell (1793–1799)*. Boston: Little, Brown and Company, 1972.

————. *George Washington: The Forge of Experience (1732–1775)*. Boston: Little, Brown and Company, 1965.

————. *George Washington and the New Nation (1783–1793)*. Boston: Little, Brown and Company, 1970.

Freeman, Douglas Southall. *George Washington, A Biography*. 6 vols. New York: Charles Scribner's Sons, 1948–1954.

Jefferson, Thomas. *Thomas Jefferson Writings*. Edited by Merrill D. Peterson. New York: The Library of America, 1984.

Ketcham, Ralph. *James Madison*. New York: The Macmillan Company, 1971.

Ketchum, Richard M. *The Winter Soldiers*. New York: Owl Books, 1999.

Leckie, Robert. *George Washington's War*. New York: HarperCollins, 1992.

Longmore, Paul K. *The Invention of George Washington*. Charlottesville: University Press of Virginia, 1999.

Martin, Joseph Plumb. *Private Yankee Doodle*. Washington, D.C.: Eastern Acorn Press, 1993.

Miller, John C. *The Federalist Era*. New York: Harper & Row, 1960.

Miller, William. *A New History of the United States*. New York: George Braziller Inc., 1958.

Morison, Samuel Eliot. *The Oxford History of the American People*. New York: Oxford University Press, 1965.

Randall, Willard Sterne. *George Washington: A Life*. New York: Henry Holt, 1997.

Rutland, Robert A. *James Madison: The Founding Father*. New York: Macmillan Publishing Company, 1987.

Schama, Simon. *Citizens: A Chronicle of the French Revolution*. New York: Alfred A. Knopf, 1989.

Scheer, George F., and Hugh F. Rankin. *Rebels & Redcoats*. New York: DaCapo Press, n.d. Reprint, Cleveland: World Pub., 1957.

Sharp, James Roger. *American Politics in the Early Republic*. New Haven: Yale University Press, 1993.

Slaughter, Thomas P. *The Whiskey Rebellion*. New York: Oxford University Press, 1986.

Smith, Page. *A New Age Now Begins: A People's History of the American Revolution*. 2 vols. 1976. Reprint, New York: Penguin, 1989.

Smith, Richard Norton. *Patriarch: George Washington and the New American Nation*. Boston: Houghton Mifflin Company, 1993.

Stokesbury, James L. *A Short History of the American Revolution*. New York: Quill, 1991.

Szatmary, David P. *Shays's Rebellion*. Amherst: University of Massachusetts Press, 1980.

Thane, Elswyth. *Washington's Lady*. 1954. Reprint, Mattituck, NY: Aeonian Press Inc., 1977.

Washington, George. *George Washington Writings*. Edited by John Rhodehamel. New York: The Library of America, 1997.

Wills, Gary. *Cincinnatus: George Washington and the Enlightenment*. Garden City, NY: Doubleday & Company, 1984.

FURTHER READING AND WEBSITES

Bliven, Bruce Jr. *The American Revolution*. New York: Random House, 2002.

Bohannon, Lisa Frederiksen. *The American Revolution*. Minneapolis: Lerner Publications Company, 2004.

Bruns, Roger. *George Washington*. New York: Chelsea House Publishers, 1987.

Canon, Jill. *Heroines of the American Revolution*. Santa Barbara, CA: Belleropon, 1998.

Fleming, Thomas J. *First in Their Hearts*. New York: Walker, 1984.

George Washington, Founding Father. Produced and directed by Adam Friedman and Monte Markham. 50 min. A&E Home Video, 1994. Videocassette.

George Washington: The Man Who Wouldn't Be King. Produced and directed by David Sutherland. Written by William Martin. 60 min. PBS Home Video, 1993. Videocassette.

George Washington's Mount Vernon. <http://www.mountvernon.org>. The official web site of Washington's Mount Vernon home. This is a place to start to learn about the first president.

Hakim, Joy. *From Colonies to Country*. New York: Oxford University Press, 1993.

Hauptly, Denis. *A Convention of Delegates*. New York: Atheneum, 1987.

Hilton, Suzanne. *The World of Young George Washington*. New York: Walker, 1987.

The Life of George Washington. Produced by Finley-Holiday Films. Written by Robert B. Gibby. 30 min. Finley-Holiday Films, 1989. Videocassette.

Marrin, Albert. *George Washington & the Founding of a Nation*. New York: Dutton Children's Books, 2001.

Meet George Washington. Produced and directed by Donald B. Hyatt. Written by Richard Hanser. 60 min. NBC News Productions; distributed by Time-Life Video, 1991. Videocassette.

Meltzer, Milton. *George Washington and the Birth of Our Nation*. New York: Franklin Watts, 1986.

Miller, Brandon Marie. *Growing Up in Revolution and the New Nation 1775 to 1800*. Minneapolis: Lerner Publications Company, 2003.

Nardo, Don. *The American Revolution*. San Diego: Greenhaven Press, 1998.

Osborne, Mary Pope. *George Washington: Leader of a New Nation*. New York: Dial Books for Young Readers, 1991.

The Papers of George Washington. <http://gwpapers.virginia.edu>. This site lets students get a firsthand look at Washington's quotations. There are links and even a Frequently Asked Questions section.

INDEX

ABOUT THE AUTHOR

Children's author Jeremy Roberts has written many books for young people, including biographies of Presidents Franklin Delano Roosevelt and Abraham Lincoln for Lerner Publications Company. Writing as Jim DeFelice, he has written a trilogy of historical novels published by St. Martin's Press set during the Revolutionary War and based on the exploits of George Washington's secret service. He and his family live in the Hudson Valley near Washington's last Revolutionary War encampment.

PHOTO ACKNOWLEDGMENTS

The images in this book are used with the permission of: North Wind Picture Archives, pp. 2, 6, 14, 16, 20, 22, 25, 29, 30, 32, 35, 43, 46, 48, 52, 53, 58, 60, 71, 74, 77 (left and right), 82, 84, 87, 89, 93, 99, 101; © Bettmann/CORBIS, p. 11; Library of Congress, pp. 13, 38, 41; Library of Congress, LC-USZ62-74107, p. 18; Laura Westlund, pp. 27, 62, 70; Yale University Library, p. 49; Library of Congress, LC-USZ62-96920, p. 50; Architect of the Capitol, p. 66.

Front cover: © Museum of the City of New York/CORBIS.